Introduction

1 Readership

Oxford English for Computing is intended for:

- students of Computer Science in technical colleges and universities
- people working with computers

  who want to improve their knowledge of English
- for study
- because they need to use English-language manuals, textbooks, and reference works
- because they plan to work in an English-speaking country

2 Objectives

Oxford English for Computing aims at all-round skills improvement:

- listening – to understand native and non-native professionals and students, talking about their work and study
  - to understand experts talking informally about aspects of computing
- speaking – to communicate about computing topics
- reading – to understand a wide variety of text including diagrams, tables, and advertisements
  - to compare different sources of information, written and spoken
- writing – to write descriptions and explanations of processes
  - to write summaries of longer texts
  - to write work-related letters

3 Authors

This book has two authors, both experienced teachers of English for computing. Care has been taken to ensure that the book is methodologically sound and at the same time that the technical content is correct and up-to-date. Recent important developments in computing are included. P Charles Brown is co-author of *English for Computer Science*, OUP.

4 Textbook design

This textbook is designed to meet the requirements of both teachers and students. The authors recognize th[...] specialist knowledge of computing. They also recognize that the students who use this book want some exposure to the kind of texts used by their fellows in English-speaking countries. The materials used in this book therefore consist of a mixture of non-technical and technical texts. Tasks that accompany the more technical passages are designed in such a way that they can be used for self-study or homework if the teacher so desires.

5 Organization

This textbook contains 15 units and 14 language focus sections designed to provide a minimum of 100 hours of work. Typically, each unit starts by examining some general area of computing or computer technology before focusing on a specific aspect or example of that general area.

The language focus sections have been adapted from *English for Computer Science, New Edition*, OUP, 1987. However, much of the original material has been updated, rewritten, or replaced.

Oxford English for Computing includes two appendices. Appendix 1, *Letter writing*, contains a complete guide to writing simple work-related letters. Appendix 2, *Glossary of technical terms and abbreviations*, consists of brief definitions of all important technical terms in this book together with abbreviations commonly used in computing.

6 Sections

Start up

This section contains starter activities. It is intended to start students thinking about the topic of the unit and to encourage them to share both relevant language and knowledge of the topic.

Reading

All units contain at least two reading passages. The first reading passage is always general in nature. The second reading passage is usually more specific and/or technical and can be used for individual study. The activities which accompany passages are designed to improve both extensive reading skills (more speed, less attention to detail) and intensives reading skills (less speed, more attention to detail). Because the texts are authentic, some difficult but non-essential words are glossed at the end of specific passages, but weaker classes may need further help from the teacher.

The following reading passages are recorded on the cassette:

Listening

Each unit has a listening section. Many of the dialogues are based on actual transcripts, though some have been simplified. The teacher should be prepared to play the tape as often as is necessary for the students to complete a particular task. In the case of weaker classes, it may be appropriate to photocopy and distribute the transcripts in the Answer Book*.

*Note: You may make photocopies of tapescripts for distribution to students, but copyright law does not normally allow multiple copying of published material.

Speaking

These activities are for fluency, practice, not accuracy. The real importance of these activities lies in the communicative process. Often students will not understand each other at first. It is important that they develop strategies for coping with not understanding and not being understood. For example, they should be encouraged to ask for clarification when they do not understand and to try rephrasing when they are not understood.

Writing

There are two kinds of writing section. One concentrates on reinforcing language. Writing tasks of this kind include descriptions, guided summaries, and reports. The other kind of writing section focuses on the translation into the mother tongue of selected paragraphs from the reading passages. Such paragraphs are chosen for grammatical or lexical content. Letter-writing skills are covered in Appendix 1 of the Student's Book.

7 Spelling

As the texts in *Oxford English for Computing* are authentic and come from a variety of sources, some inconsistencies in spelling and punctuation will be found. The publishers have not attempted to standardize these, since students will be exposed to such inconsistencies in their professional lives. Certain words deserve special mention. In British texts on computing the American spelling *analog* is fast becoming standard, whereas the British texts on electronics *analogue* is almost always used. The spelling of *disk/disc* varies widely. The usual forms are: *compact disc*; *hard/floppy disk*, *disk drive*, etc.

1

Personal Computing

Task 1 [p.4]

Alone, in pairs, or in small groups of three or four, students identify the devices and then tell the class what each one is used for.

Answers

a Mouse: an input device connected by a wire to the computer. When the mouse is moved, the cursor will move along the screen in the same direction in which the mouse is being moved.

b Stylus: a pen-like input device connected by a wire to the computer. A stylus replaces the keyboard. It is used to write directly on the screen to input data.

c Joy-stick: an input device especially helpful when playing computer games. The joy-stick can be used to control the movements of objects displayed on the screen.

d Magnetic card reader: a device that can read the card on which information has been magnetically recorded.

Task 2 [pp.4–5]

The teacher plays the tape once and asks the students to complete the table.

Suggestion 1 Play the tape a second time, if necessary. In pairs, students take turns reporting the information to each other.

Suggestion 2 In pairs, students report to each other the information they have recorded. They may complete the table with the information they receive from each other. If not, play the tape a second time. In a new pair, each student reports the information from the table.

The students then check with the teacher at class level, listening to appropriate parts of the tape again.

Tapescript

Interview 1

INTERVIEWER: Excuse me, sir. I'm doing some market research on visitors to the *Computer World* exhibition. Could you spare me a few minutes to answer some simple questions?

JOHN: OK. Provided that it doesn't take too long.

INTERVIEWER: Thanks very much. It won't take long, I promise. First, what is your name?

JOHN: John Steele.

INTERVIEWER: Could you spell your surname, please?

JOHN: S-T-E-E-L-E.

INTERVIEWER: And what do you do, Mr Steele?

JOHN: I'm a computer consultant.

INTERVIEWER: And what exactly do you do as a computer consultant?

JOHN: Advise customers – usually companies – that want to computerize certain procedures.

INTERVIEWER: Could you give me an example?

JOHN: Of course. I recently did some work for a company that wanted to computerize all their bookkeeping. I advised them on the best hardware to buy and I developed a software package to suit their needs.

INTERVIEWER: What hardware do you use?

JOHN: I use an IBM PC.

INTERVIEWER: Why IBM?

JOHN: Because I know them well. I bought an IBM ten years ago for my personal use, I've been using one ever since.

INTERVIEWER: Is it simply a question of habit, then?

JOHN: No. I also know lots of other IBM users that I exchange ideas with. And of course there's a lot of software available.

INTERVIEWER: Do you ever advise your customers to buy Macintoshes?

JOHN: (*laughs*) Sometimes. It depends on what kind of application the customer wants to run.

INTERVIEWER: Mr Steele, thank you very much.

Interview 2

INTERVIEWER: Excuse me, sir. I'm doing some market research on visitors to the *Computer World* exhibition. Could you spare me a few minutes to answer some simple questions?

ENRIQUE: No problem.

INTERVIEWER: First, what's your name and what do you do?

ENRIQUE: My name is Enrique Vargas and I'm a student.

INTERVIEWER: Sorry, how do you spell your name?

1

ENRIQUE: E-N-R-I-Q-U-E, Vargas: V-A-R-G-A-S.

INTERVIEWER: And where are you studying, Enrique? May I call you Enrique?

ENRIQUE: Yes, of course. I study Computer Science at the Monterrey Institute of Technology in Mexico.

INTERVIEWER: Do you own a PC?

ENRIQUE: Yes, I have an Apple Macintosh.

INTERVIEWER: Why did you choose a Mac as opposed to an IBM or an IBM clone?

ENRIQUE: I think Macs are easier to use than IBM PCs. I use the mouse feature a lot, which is standard on all Macs. Then there's the graphical user interface and the windows.

INTERVIEWER: Graphical user interface? Could you explain that?

ENRIQUE: Well, put simply, it means that you click on icons instead of typing in commands.

INTERVIEWER: I see. You mentioned windows. Doesn't IBM also use windows?

ENRIQUE: Yes, but I think their windows are harder to set up. In any case, I'm used to the Mac.

INTERVIEWER: Thank you very much for talking to me, Enrique.

ENRIQUE: It's my pleasure.

Answers

	Interview 1	Interview 2
Name:	*John Steele*	*Enrique Vargas*
Occupation:	*Computer Consultant*	*Student*
Type of PC used:	*IMB PC*	*Apple Macintosh*
Reasons for choice:	1 *knows them well*	1 *easier to use*
	2 *exchanges information with other users*	2 *GUI – click on icons/no typing in commands*
	3 *a lot of software available*	3 *windows easier to set up*

Task 3 [p.5]

Alone or in pairs, students fill in the blanks, then listen to the tape to complete the text or to check answers.

Answers

1	choose	5	standard	9	up
2	clone	6	icons	10	used
3	easier	7	commands	11	to
4	mouse	8	set		

Task 4 [p.5]

Alone or in pairs, students try to match each word with the correct definition. They then discuss it at class level.

Answers

1 c	3 f	5 g	7 b
2 e	4 a	6 d	

Task 5 [p.6]

Suggestion 1 Alone, students read the text and then write a suitable title. In pairs or groups of three, they discuss their choices.

Suggestion 2 Alone, students read and complete text and then, in pairs or small groups, they decide on a suitable title.

The teacher may ask the class to justify their choices.

Example answers

The History of Personal Computing/The Development of the Personal Computer

Task 6 [p.7]

Suggestion 1 Alone, students check off which strategies they have used.

Suggestion 2 In pairs or in groups of three, students can discuss the appropriateness or inappropriateness of each strategy.

The teacher can elicit responses from students and then explain which strategies are the most or least appropriate.

Answers

Statement 2 is the most appropriate because the task only required the student to understand the main topic of the text, not specific points or facts. Statement 1 would not be an appropriate strategy for a first reading, and Statements 3 and 4 are appropriate strategies for summarizing.

Task 7 [p.7]

Alone or in pairs, students can write the answers to the questions, making sure they know where the information can be found in the text, and check the answers with the teacher. The teacher can elicit responses to check the answers.

Answers

1 Four.
2 70,000,000.
3 Xerox Corporation.
4 Apple.
5 Users type in commands to perform a function.
6 Digital Research disk operating system.
7 c.
8 Microchips in washing-machines and cars; books may not be published in paper form; information available world-wide.

Task 8 [p.7]

Alone or in pairs, students can find the answers, then check with another student and with the teacher.

Answers

1 world-wide
2 challenged
3 mistakes
4 funded
5 purchase
6 initial
7 endorsement
8 upgraded

Task 9 [p.7]

Suggestion 1 Alone, students translate the text.

Suggestion 2 In pairs, students translate the text, then pass it on to another pair for editing. Finally, the pairs get together to discuss the editing.

Students give their translations to the teacher for correction.

The teacher may take this opportunity to discuss translation problems and techniques.

Task 10 [p.7]

Suggestion 1 Alone, students make a list to then discuss in small groups.

Suggestion 2 Students individually make a list to then discuss with a partner. The pairs discuss their respective lists and add new information. They then form groups of four by combining two pairs and repeat the exercise. The teacher may regroup as often as necessary.

Example Answers

1 For word processing, to access bulletin boards, to access computers at work, to compose music, for household accounts, for educational software. (Although the UK has more PCs at home per household than any other country in the world, most of them are used for playing games.)

The processor

Task 11 [p.8]

Alone or in pairs, students fill in the gaps. With another student or pair, they discuss the answers. The students then check with the teacher at class level.

Answers

1 system board
2 microprocessor
3 conductive
4 buses
5 adaptor boards
6 input or output devices
7 clock
8 accumulators
9 registers

Task 12 [p.9]

Suggestion 1 Alone, students match the terms with the appropriate explanation or definition. Answers are checked by the teacher at class level.

Suggestion 2 Make pairs or groups of three students, and ask them to work together. Make new pairs or new groups and repeat the activity. The teacher need only deal with the terms that are still causing problems.

Answers

1 b	4 h	7 e
2 g	5 a	8 i
3 d	6 c	9 f

Task 13 [p.10]

Students work in pairs for this speaking practice, changing partners as often as necessary.

Task 14 [p.10]

Students can work individually or in pairs on this revision activity.

Answers

Across

1 channel	5 firmware	9 database
2 icon	6 mouse	10 window
3 joystick	7 control unit	11 address bus
4 output	8 megabyte	

Down

12 accumulator

Language Focus A

Contextual reference

All the exercises in Language focus sections may be done individually or in pairs. The teacher should go through the content of the section carefully at class level.

Exercise 1 [p.11]

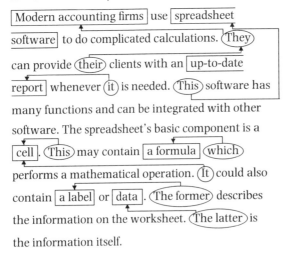

Modern accounting firms use spreadsheet software to do complicated calculations. They can provide their clients with an up-to-date report whenever it is needed. This software has many functions and can be integrated with other software. The spreadsheet's basic component is a cell. This may contain a formula which performs a mathematical operation. It could also contain a label or data. The former describes the information on the worksheet. The latter is the information itself.

The worksheet is the basic work area of a spreadsheet program. It is made up of cells arranged in rows and columns. The number of these varies depending on the software you are using. You can change the width and format of cells. Such parameters are usually quite easy to change with just a few keystrokes.

Exercise 2 [p.12]

1 PCs
2 Xerox Corporation
3 the operating system developed for Apple's computers
4 the first IBM PC
5 command-based operating systems
6 Digital Research
7 the original IBM PC minimum of 16K of memory

2

Portable Computers

Task 1 [p.13]

Suggestion 1 The teacher asks individual students for their opinions and writes the information on the board.

Suggestion 2 In pairs or in small groups, students discuss questions and take notes. In new pairs or groups, any new information can be added to each student's notes. This can be repeated as often as necessary. Afterwards, the teacher can elicit information from the students and write it on the board.

Example answers

1 The size of a general-purpose computer will ultimately be limited by the input and output method used. There are practical limitations on how small a keyboard may become and still be used. Similarly, if a screen is too small, it either will not display enough information, or the information displayed will be too small to read easily. Other forms of input, such as pen-based computers may, in the future, allow for smaller computers than those with keyboards. Thus, it is not the size of the chip that is the limiting factor on the size of the computer, but the human factor.

2 The first computers made with valves in the 1940s took up most of a building and did not have much more computing power than the first PCs. Large mainframes may require air- or even water-cooling to dissipate the heat generated by the chips. Technology is addressing this with more efficient chips. As computers have become smaller, size tends to be important if you want to put the computer inside something like a car. If the computers on Concorde were replaced with modern ones, it would be possible to fit eight more passenger seats. Other examples of computers in which size plays an important part include hand-held computers, digital watches, missile systems, space shuttles, automatic cameras, and domestic appliances.

Task 2 [p.14]

Play the tape once and ask the students to complete the table individually.

Note that *pounds* and *inches* are used in the USA and Canada, and, less often, in the UK. 1 pound (1lb) = 0.45 kg; 1 inch (1") = 25.4 mm.

Suggestion 1 Play the tape a second time, if necessary. In pairs, students then take turns reporting the information to each other.

Suggestion 2 Students complete the table in pairs. Then, in a new pair, each student reports the information from the table.

The students then check with the teacher at class level.

Tapescript

HOST: Sandra, many of our listeners have written to us asking us to talk about portable computers. I hope you'll be able to clarify things for us.

SANDRA: I hope so, too. The first point to make is that portable computers are simply smaller versions of desktop computers. They are as versatile, reliable, and fast as any computer on your desk.

HOST: But then why are some referred to as laptops, others as notebooks, and still others as palmtops? What's the difference?

SANDRA: Simply put, portables are larger than laptops, laptops are larger than notebooks, and notebooks are larger than palmtops. In other words, it's a question of physical size and weight.

HOST: Are there any other characteristics that differentiate them?

SANDRA: Yes. For instance, portable computers can only run on AC power. Like desktop computers, they must be plugged in. They weigh between fifteen and twenty pounts and have a screen that's at least ten inches diagonally.

HOST: How do laptops compare with this?

SANDRA: Laptops are smaller than portables, and most of them can fit into a briefcase. They don't need to be plugged in; they operate on rechargeable batteries. Most weigh between eight and fifteen pounds and have a screen which is about ten inches diagonally.

HOST: What about notebooks?

SANDRA: Well, notebooks weigh less and can have smaller screens. Some weigh as little as four pounds. The smallest screen I've seen is about eight inches diagonally. Notebooks are also thinner than laptops, but they work just as well.

HOST: Now that we know the basic differences between portables, laptops, and notebooks, what are clipboards?

SANDRA: Clipboards, as the name implies, look like a clipboard or a slate. They can operate with rechargeable batteries and are very thin, weighing between three and six pounds at the most. Their screen size is similar to laptops and notebooks, but one important feature is that they don't have a keyboard. They use a pen or stylus.

HOST: You mean to say that you don't have to type in letters or numbers!

SANDRA: Exactly. All you need is a pen that you use to print on the screen. That's why they call them pen-based computers.

HOST: That's incredible!

SANDRA: Now, I didn't mention palmtops. Palmtop computers, or hand-held computers as they are also known, are so small that they can fit in your hand. They weigh less than one pound. Of course, they have a very small screen, but they can operate on alkaline batteries. Most people use these as agenda books, phone books, or address books.

Answers

1	AC power	8	rechargeable
2	20	9	3
3	**Laptop**	10	pen or stylus
4	batteries	11	**Palmtop**
5	10 inches	12	alkaline
6	four	13	1 pound
7	8 inches		

Task 3 [p.15]

Alone or in pairs, students try to match each word with the correct definition. The teacher checks their answers at class level.

Answers

a 7   b 6   c 1   d 5   e 2   f 4   g 3

Task 4 [pp.15–16]

Alone, students read the text, and then, in pairs or groups of three, discuss the title *Delete Keys* and suggest better ones.

Example answers

The title is a play on words. The 'delete key' is the key on a keyboard which enables the user to erase information on screen. The title is also an imperative: *Delete* (i.e. *Forget about*) *Keys* – (*we now have*) *Clipboard Technology*. An alternative title could be *From Keyboard to Clipboard*.

Task 5 [p.16]

Suggestion 1 Alone or in pairs, students decide whether the statements are true or false and identify where they think the information appears in the text to justify their answers. They then make the necessary changes to the false statements.

The teacher then elicits responses around the class to check, making sure students can give line references to support their answers.

Suggestion 2 Make this an interactive reading task, following the procedure described below. (This approach can be used by the teacher for any intensive reading exercise. It is not appropriate for a task requiring the student to understand only the general meaning.)

In pairs or in groups of three, students silently read the text, one paragraph at a time. After each paragraph, the students close their books and tell each other the information they have read. The listener(s) in the group can add information that has been missed. They each take turns until the complete text has been done in the students' own words. Then, together, they decide on appropriate answers to the questions.

Answers

1 F
2 F (it has been in development for 20 years according to the text)
3 T
4 T
5 F (but you could argue that, because the text says it happens after 1/3 second, *a fortiori* this will be true after 1/2 second)
6 T
7 F
8 F

Task 6 [p.17]

Alone or in pairs, students decide what to write and show where they think the information appears in the text to justify their answers. Then, new pairs can be formed and the activity can be repeated.

The teacher elicits responses around the class to check answers.

Example answers

1 No, biggger than an actual clipboard.
2 No, it has a stylus.
3 You print directly on the screen.
4 When the tip does not touch the screen.
5 The recognition software identifies the letters and numbers.
6 You draw a line through it.
7 Not yet, but they will be soon.

Task 7 [p.17]

Alone or in pairs, students find the answers, then check their answers with other students or with the teacher.

Answers

1 machines
2 technologies
3 the stylus
4 the tip does not touch the screen for a third of a second or more
5 the computer's pattern recognition software
6 computer
7 clipboard systems . . . quirks of a particular user's printing
8 the designers of clipboard computers

Task 8 [p.17]

Alone or in pairs, students find the answers, then check their answers with other students or with the teacher.

Answers

1 figure out
2 marketed
3 coating
4 coordinates
5 connect
6 smoothing out
7 crooked
8 errant
9 flick
10 quirk

Task 9 [p.18]

Alone or in pairs, students find the answers, then check their answers with another student or pair or with the teacher.

Answers

1a *electronic*
 b *electronically*
 c *electronics*
2a *technological*
 b *technologies*
 c *technologically*
3a *identifies*
 b *identity*
 c *identifying*
4a *computerization*
 b *compute*
 c *computations*

Task 10 [p.18]

Suggestion 1 Alone, students translate the text.

Suggestion 2 In pairs, students translate the text, then pass it on to another pair for editing. Finally, the pairs get together to discuss the editing.

Students give their translations to the teacher for correction.

The teacher may take this opportunity to discuss translation problems and techniques.

Task 11 [p.18]

Students individually make a list of points to discuss in pairs or small groups. Let them discuss their respective lists and add information they have heard. They then make the groups bigger by combining two pairs or small groups, and repeat the exercise. The teacher may regroup as often as necessary.

Example answers

1 Some limitations of portable computers are: battery life; weight; size of screen; size of keyboard for touch-typist; difficulties of using a mouse when travelling; quality of the display.

Task 12 [p.19]

Suggestion 1 Students work individually, then hand in their written work to be corrected by the teacher.

Suggestion 2 Students can work in pairs to write their advertisement, then they can share their work with another pair for editing purposes before giving it to the teacher for checking.

Task 13 [p.20]

The teacher could provide some key-language choral, pronunciation, and stress practice before students begin this task. He/She should go around the class helping and giving guidance where necessary. Students should be working in pairs. Once they have done the activity they may form a new pair and do it again.

The teacher may decide to repeat this activity at a later date for revision or as a warm-up activity.

Operating systems

Task 14 [pp.20–21]

Suggestion 1 Students can answer the questions individually when called upon by the teacher.

Suggestion 2 Working in pairs, students can discuss the questions, then regroup in new pairs to repeat the activity. Regrouping can occur as often as necessary.

Students then read the text to check the answers and either discuss in pairs or groups, or discuss with the teacher.

Example answers

1 An operating system is a master control system which controls the functions of the computer system and the application programs.
2 The operating system is stored on disk and has to be loaded into the internal memory (RAM) by the start-up process ('booting').
3 Balancing system resources between different applications, controlling printing, controlling disk access and file locking, controlling terminals in a multi-user environment, handling the use of memory by the programs running, monitoring hardware failures.

Task 15 [p.22]

Suggestion 1 Alone, students read the text again and then write suitable answers to the questions.

Suggestion 2 Treat this as an interactive reading task, following the procedure described in Suggestion 2, Task 5 (Unit 2), on page 6. The teacher rounds up ideas at class level.

Answers

1 Because some software is only designed to run under the control of specific operating systems.
2 Processing several application programs concurrently.
3 Payroll calculations, accounting transaction updates, bank interest calculations, statement printing, label printing, and cheque processing.

Task 16 [p.22]

Alone or in pairs, students fill in the gaps, forming new pairs or working with another student to check their answers. The teacher should ensure that students use only the prompts given. If the teacher is not satisfied that everyone has the correct information, he/she can go through it at class level.

Answers

1 monitor
2 monitor
3 diagnose
4 format
5 monitor
6 execute/monitor
7 diagnose
8 execute

Task 17 [p.22]

Alone or in pairs, students match the DOS commands with the appropriate explanation, forming new pairs, or working with another student to check their answers.

If necessary, the teacher can go through at class level.

Answers

1 d
2 e
3 j
4 f
5 i
6 g
7 c
8 b
9 a
10 h

Task 18 [p.23]

Students work individually and then check with another student or with the teacher at class level.

Answers

1 palmtop
2 stylus
3 delete
4 clipboard
5 data
6 grid
7 interrupt
8 template
9 pixel

Language focus B

Word-formation: prefixes

Exercise 2 [pp.26–27]

1 **in**expensive (not), **re**usable (do again)
2 **mal**functions (bad), **inter**face (between, among)
3 **multi**plexor (many), **dis**connected (opposite action)
4 **im**proper (not), **anti**glare (against), **im**possible (not)
5 **re**format (do again)
6 **maxi**mize (large), **bi**lingual (two), **tri**lingual (three)
7 **in**put, **out**put
8 **retro**active (backward), **bi**annual (two)
9 **oct**al (eight), **hex**adecimal (six), **bi**nary (two)
10 **ir**regular (not), **re**written (do again)

Exercise 3 [p.27]

1 mono
2 Sub
3 mega
4 de
5 semi
6 multi
7 dec
8 inter

3

Online services

Task 1 [p.28]

Suggestion 1 The teacher can ask individual students for their opinions and write the information on the board.

Suggestion 2 In pairs or in small groups, students can discuss each question and take notes. Then, new pairs or groups can be formed and new information can be added to each student's notes. This can be repeated as often as necessary. Afterwards, the teacher can elicit information from the students and write it on the board.

Example answers

1 Compuserve is a US-based facility, but it is accessible through local calls in many parts of the world, including Europe. Minitel is an example of a French online service. ITAPAC is an example of an Italian online service.

2 Online services may provide the following facilities: bulletin boards (electronic noticeboard for leaving messages and replies accessible to everyone), shopping by post, e-mail, databases, software tools, and software updates.

Task 2 [pp.28–29]

Suggestion 1 The teacher can ask students, alone or in pairs, to predict the answers, using their own knowledge of online services. The students then read the text and check their answers.

Suggestion 2 Alone or in pairs, students read the passage and decide whether the statements are true or false.

The teacher then checks answers at class level, making sure students can give line references to support their answers.

Answers

1 T
2 T
3 F ('Judge it based on what it offers and how it meets your needs – not in comparison to what you're used to using.')
4 T
5 F (Bix is owned by McGraw-Hill)
6 F (is moderated by = is run by) although students could argue that the information is not given in the text, so it is neither true nor false
7 F
8 F (The article implies that two more services have been added, not that they are the only two.)

Task 3 [p.30]

Alone or in pairs, students fill in the gaps, check their answers with another student, then check with the teacher.

Answers

1 particular	5 better
2 favourite	6 correspond
3 advantages	7 interlinked
4 unique	8 continue

Task 4 [p.30]

Suggestion 1 Alone, students circle their choices and write/give reasons.

Suggestion 2 In pairs or in groups of three, students can discuss the choices they have made and give reasons.

The teacher can elicit responses from each group or individual, then explain which are the correct answers.

Answers

1 **c** (because of the use of contractions, the vocabulary, the direct approach to 'you' the idiomatic language, the informal link words, such as 'still' and 'so', the use of 'And' to open a sentence, sentences without a verb, etc.)

2 **a** or **d** (because of the high frequency of acronyms, the detailed information, etc. The information is too specific, and the style is too 'spoken', for a general magazine or newspaper.)

Task 5 [p.30]

Alone or in pairs, students find the answers, check them with another student or pair, then check with the teacher.

Answers

2	*dis*	**5**	*dis/un*	**7**	*im*
3	*dis*	**6**	*un*	**8**	*un*
4	*un*				

Task 6 [p.30]

Alone or in pairs, students find the answers, check them with another student or pair, then check with the teacher.

Answers

1 b   2 c   3 d   4 e   5 a   6 f

Task 7 [p.31]

Play the tape once and ask the students to complete the table with the missing information.

Suggestion 1 Play the tape a second time, if necessary. Place students in pairs and ask them to take turns reporting to each other the information from the table.

Suggestion 2 In pairs, students report to each other the information they have recorded. They may complete the table with the information they receive from each other. If not, play the tape a second time. In a new pair, each student reports the information from the table.

The students then check with the teacher at class level.

Tapescript

Jean-Yves Martin, a French computer technician, explains the Minitel system to Paul Burgess, an English reporter.

PAUL BURGESS:: So, Jean-Yves, what exactly is Minitel?

JEAN-YVES MARTIN: The best description I've heard, Paul, is that it's a telephone you can write with. It's a small computer terminal, linked to the telephone network, which enables users to exchange information with each other and, more importantly, to have access to hundreds of different sources of information.

PAUL BURGESS: Such as?

JEAN-YVES MARTIN: Oh, all sorts of things: weather forecasts, train schedules, home-shopping services, stock-market figures. You name it, it's available on Minitel. Oh, and there is 'Minitel rose', of course – er, 'pink Minitel', I suppose you'd say in English.

PAUL BURGESS: What's that?

JEAN-YVES MARTIN: It's a sort of rendez-vous service, a way for people to meet each other and communicate online, quite anonymously if they wish. It can get very interesting sometimes!

PAUL BURGESS: I can imagine. How did the system start?

JEAN-YVES MARTIN: It began in 1982. As an experiment, the PTT – which ran telecommunications in France before France Telecom split from the Post Office – put about a million Minitels into people's homes instead of printed telephone directories.

PAUL BURGESS: Did the first users have to pay for them?

JEAN-YVES MARTIN: At first not at all, or else they paid a nominal sum. Anyway, the users soon became used to the system, and started to look at some of the other services provided on Minitel. The whole thing grew from there.

PAUL BURGESS: Why do you think it became so successful?

JEAN-YVES MARTIN: Well, it doesn't cost much, it's very easy to use, and it's readily available. I think that, in the early days, these advantages outweighed all the disadvantages of the system, such as the rather primitive graphics system, the slow transmission speed, and the keyboard design which made it impossible to type really fast.

PAUL BURGESS: What plans do you have to develop Minitel in the future?

JEAN-YVES MARTIN: Well, we already have the possibility of adding a smart-card reader to the system, so that users can make bank and stock-market transactions from their home. Another possibility is portable Minitel, linked on broadband radio channels, which users can operate from their cars. The possibilities for development are endless.

PAUL BURGESS: They certainly are. Well, thank you for explaining it to me.

JEAN-YVES MARTIN: It's my pleasure. I wonder if you'd like to see . . .

Answers

1 train schedules
4 stock market figures

2 easy to use
3 readily available

2 slow transmission speed
3 keyboard design

1 a smart-card reader
2 portable Minitel

Task 8 [p.31]

Alone or in pairs, students can answer the questions and then check with another student or pair or with the teacher for the correct answers.

Answers

1 A rendez-vous service.
2 1982.
3 1,000,000.
4 No, or only a nominal sum.

Data transmission

Task 9 [p.32]

Alone or in groups of three, students can match the information from columns 1, 2, and 3 and solve the jigsaw.

They can find a partner or regroup and repeat the activity to check their answers or check with the teacher.

Answers

1 An acoustic coupler converts the electrical signal from the computer into a coded sound signal which is picked up by the telephone microphone. It then works as a modem.
2 A modem can convert a digital bit stream into an analog signal over an analog communication channel (telephone circuit). It then converts incoming analog signals back into digital signals.
3 A cluster controller may control several terminals in one location, connecting each of them to a modem. This connection is made on a shared line basis.
4 A multiplexor receives multiple signals from various terminals and combines them in dataframes for transmission on a single high-speed line to the computer. In the computer the dataframes are then separated again.
5 A gateway interconnects two or more networks, enabling data transfers to be made. It may act as a translator between incompatible networks, protocols, or software.

Task 10 [p.33]

Alone or in groups of three, students can fill in the gaps in the diagram.

They can then find a partner or regroup and repeat the activity to check their answers.

They then check with the teacher.

Answers

1 analog	5 cluster controller
2 modem	6 terminal
3 multiplexor	7 digital
4 computer	

Task 11 [p.34]

Alone or in pairs, students can try to answer the questions without first reading the text. After reading the text, they can check their answers and complete them, indicating the parts of the text that contain the answers.

Students then check with the teacher at class level.

Answers

1 There are a number, including higher speed transmission, lower incidence of error, and the facility for mixing data.
2 Analog transmission: the transmission of electrical signals represented by continuous variations in wave forms. Digital transmission: the transmission of a series of electrical on/off pulses in binary code.
3 Characters, transmission control signals, information separators, and device control.

Task 12 [p.34]

Students work in pairs following the instructions for **Student A** and **B** to describe the diagrams. The diagram being described should be covered up by the student who is listening to ensure that the description is adequate.

Task 13 [p.35]

Suggestion 1 Alone, students can write a paragraph and then have it checked by the teacher or edited by another student before giving it to the teacher.

Suggestion 2 Students can write in pairs, then share their paragraph with another pair, discussing how they could edit their information, before giving it to the teacher for correction.

Extra information

An analog signal works like a sound wave and is the basis of telephone systems. A digital signal consists of a series of bits, i.e. on/off states. The pattern of these may be converted to an analog signal and vice versa. As an analogy, think of speech converted to morse code, or of telegraph, which uses the analog telephone line to transmit a digital signal. This conversion from digital to analog may be done by a variety of methods: frequency modulation, amplitude modulation, or phase modulation.

Task 14 [p.35]

Across

Down

sav(ings) (n) in the long run.

10 Software develop(ers) (n) are producing increasing(ly) (adv) sophisticat(ed) (adj) applicat(ions) (n) for a grow(ing) (adj) glob(al) (adj) market.

*part of the noun phrase *Turning your office into a paperless environment*

Language Focus C

Word formation: suffixes

Exercise 2 [pp.37–38]

Note that the endings *-ed*, and *-ing* are not marked as suffixes when the word they belong to is being used as a verb or part of a verb.

Answers

2 A systems anal(yst) (n) studies organiz(ation)al (adj) systems and decides what act(ion) (n) needs to be taken to maxim(ize) (v) efficien(cy) (n).

3 Laser print(ers) (n) are prefer(able) (adj) to other types of print(ing) (adj) devices because of their speed and quiet(ness) (n).

4 The microcomput(er) (n) we have purchased does not have a FORTRAN compil(er) (n). It is programm(able) (adj) in BASIC only.

5 We have found that operat(ors) (n) who have the free(dom) (n) to take short breaks during the day great(ly) (adj) improve their perform(ance) (n).

6 The number of ship(ments) (n) will increase over the com(ing) (adj) months.

7 We decided to computer(ize) (v) the entire plant to give each divis(ion) (n) more independ(ence) (n).

8 Spool(ing) (n) is a way of storing data temporar(ily) (adv) on disk or tape until it can be processed by another part of the system.

9 Turn(ing) (gerund*) your office into a paper(less) (adj) environ(ment) (n) may be expens(ive) (adj) at the beginn(ing) (n) but can produce big

Programming and languages

Task 1 [p.39]

Suggestion 1 Ask the students to look at the facsimiles of the programs to identify the programming languages, then to tell the class what they are.

Suggestion 2 Put the students in groups of three or four. Ask them to identify the programming languages shown and to give reasons for their answers. Then, one member from each group reports to the class.

Answers

a C   **b** BASIC   **c** COBOL

Task 2 [pp.40–41]

The teacher asks students individually or in pairs to fill in the blanks with the missing information by predicting, using their own knowledge of programming languages. The students then read the passage and check their answers. Finally, the teacher checks answers at class level.

Answers

1 source program
2 machine code
3 applications program
4 object program, object module
5 compiler
6 linkage editor
7 load module

Task 3 [p.42]

Alone, or in pairs or groups of three, students can formulate the appropriate questions on the text and have them checked by the teacher. Then, they can work with a partner or regroup and repeat the activity until the teacher is satisfied. The teacher need only clarify those questions which are troublesome. The teacher may take this opportunity to revise question formation.

Example answers

1 Is COBOL used for scientific purposes?
2 Why was C developed in the 1970s?
3 What do you call a program written in a high-level language designed to perform a specific task?
4 Which part of the systems software converts the source code to machine code?
5 What does the linkage editor do?
6 Are software packages only sold by the hardware manufacturer?

Task 4 [p.42]

Alone, or in pairs or groups of three, students can complete the table. Students can find a partner or regroup and tell each other the information, using their table as a guide. Students then check their information with the teacher at class level.

Language	Developed	Function	Characteristic
FORTRAN	1954	*scientific and mathematical problems*	*algebraic formulae and English phrases*
COBOL	1959	*commercial purposes*	*English statements*
ALGOL	1960	mathematical and scientific purposes	*originally called International Algebraic Language*
PL/I	1964	*data processing and scientific applications*	combines features of COBOL and ALGOL
BASIC	1965	*general-purpose language*	*simple, developed for students*
C	1970s	to support Unix operating system	*highly portable*
APL	1962		
PASCAL	1971		

Task 5 [p.42]

Alone or in pairs, students can complete this activity by referring back to the text for the correct line reference. Then, they can check their answers with another student or pair, or with the teacher.

Answers

1	51–53	**3**	7–9	**5**	39–40
2	60	**4**	58		

Task 6 [p.43]

1 Computers
2 a source program
3 a program written in one of these high-level languages (is) designed to do a specific type of work
4 Institutions
5 these programs
6 compiler
7 a true systems program
8 systems routines
9 software packages
10 magnetic tapes or disks

Task 7 [p.43]

1 transformed   4 conform to
2 commission   5 corresponds to
3 fetches

Task 8 [pp.43–44]

Alone or in pairs, students can find the answers and check them with another student or pair, or with the teacher.

Answers

1a	*instructor*	**3a**	*resulting*
b	*instructed*	**b**	*results*
c	*instruction*	**4a**	*specific*
2a	*compiler*	**b**	*specific/specified*
b	*compiles*	**c**	*specifications*
c	*compiled*		

C Language

Task 9 [p.44]

Alone or in pairs, students decide whether the statements are true or false by predicting, using their own knowledge of C.

The teacher then plays the tape, and students check their predictions against what they hear.

Alone or in pairs, students decide whether the statements are true or false and make the necessary changes to the false statements. Then, with another student or pair, the activity can be repeated before the teacher elicits responses from students to check the answers at class level.

Students may find this listening passage difficult because of the terminology used. Teachers may wish to pre-teach some of this, referring to the glossary if necessary.

Tapescript

INTERVIEWER: C was originally written to support the development of the UNIX operating system. Is that right?

DAVID WENDT: Yes, that's right. Dennis Ritchie designed C in the early 1970s and UNIX is written in C. However, it's actually the result of a development process that began with a language called BCPL, which was developed in 1967.

INTERVIEWER: So C is based on BCPL?

DAVID WENDT: Indirectly, yes. Ken Thompson, the developer of UNIX, had been using both assembly language and a language called B. C evolved from B and BCPL. In 1973, Ritchie and Thompson rewrote UNIX in C.

INTERVIEWER: C was used almost exclusively for systems programming to begin with, so why has it become so popular as a general purpose language?

DAVID WENDT: Well, it's true that it was – and still is – used for systems programming. Much of MS/DOS and OS/2, and of course UNIX, is written in C. However, when UNIX became one of the most popular multi-user operating systems, C was adopted by programmers for almost any programming task.

INTERVIEWER: But what do you think makes C more attractive than, say PASCAL?

DAVID WENDT: C's main attraction is that it has a small but very powerful set of operators. It combines the power of Assembler with the elegance of high-level languages.

INTERVIEWER: Could you give some examples of how it does that?

DAVID WENDT: Yes. With C, the programmer can access the underlying hardware. He can access memory addresses directly, he can perform operations on values stored as bits, and he can store variables in registers, just as in Assembler. This produces faster and more efficient code than is produced by high-level languages like PASCAL. At the same time, it provides the fundamental control flow constructs required for well-structured programs: decision-making, loops, and subprograms. These features combined together provide a very powerful tool for the programmer.

INTERVIEWER: You make it sound like the ideal language for everyone.

DAVID WENDT: Well, no, I'm not saying that. But if you need to write programs that are compact, fast in execution, and yet portable from one computer to another, then C is the language you should be using.

INTERVIEWER: One last point: you said earlier that C was the result of a development process. Is this development continuing? I mean, are we going to see a language called D?

DAVID WENDT: (*laughs*) As you know, nothing stands still in the field of computing. There is a language C++ which has developed from C, and its use is increasing. Things are definitely moving to object-orientated programming. Language like C++ and Smalltalk are the languages of the next decade (*pause*) as are functional languages, but that's another story.

Answers

1 F
2 F
3 T
4 F
5 T
6 F (the speaker says that C *combines the power of Assembler...* but does not say that it is more powerful)
7 T
8 F
9 F
10 F

Task 10 [p.45]

Alone or in pairs, students try to fill in the missing words. The teacher then plays the tape, and students check their answers. The teacher then checks answers at class level.

Answers

1	bits	4	subprogram
2	efficient	6	compact
3	control flow	7	portable

Task 11 [pp.45–46]

Alone or in pairs, students can fill in the gaps with the appropriate word(s) after reading the text. They can check their answers with others or with the teacher.

Answers

1	main	6	braces
2	comment	7	terminator
3	declaration	8	compiler/syntax
4	three	9	variable
5	four and five	10	type declaration

Task 12 [p.47]

Alone or in pairs, students can find the words in the text with similar meanings, then check their answers with another student or pair or with the teacher.

Answers

1	braces	4	identified
2	variable	5	terminated
3	scan	6	initial

Task 13 [p.47]

Alone or in pairs, students can complete the table, then check their answers with each other or with the teacher.

Answers

1	less than	4	equal to or greater than
2	<=	5	not equal to
3	greater than		

Task 14 [p.47]

Alone or in pairs, students can complete the table by writing the appropriate sentences. Then, they can check their answers with another student or pair, or with the teacher.

Answers

1 a is not equal to b
2 a is greater than b
3 a is equal to or less than b
4 a is equal to or greater than b
5 a is less than b
6 a is equal to b

Task 15 [p.47]

Suggestion 1 The teacher gives the students time to make notes individually or in pairs, then initiates a class discussion.

Suggestion 2 The teacher divides the class into two. One half of the class prepares notes to defend the first statement. The other half prepares notes to defend the second statement (students should not be allowed to choose which statement they defend). In a large class, the two halves can first be divided into smaller groups to make notes. These smaller groups can then get together with the other groups in their half of the class to produce one set of notes. The class can then debate the issue.

Extra information

At a superficial level, programming languages and natural languages are similar. Programming languages have grammatical rules that need to be learnt, just as natural languages do. At the same level, computers can 'understand' and 'communicate with' humans through programming languages: superficial interaction is possible. However, programming languages are data-free and therefore contain no information in themselves. The information is contained in the data which is processed, but is independent of the language which is used to write the commands to proceed it. The sole purpose of a programming language is to give instructions to a computer, which – providing they are syntactically correct – will be executed. A syntactically correct statement in a programming language has only one interpretation. By definition, it cannot be ambiguous. You cannot make jokes in computer languages.

Task 16 [p.48]

1	high-level	f	language
2	machine	h	code
3	systems	j	routine
4	object	e	module
5	linkage	g	editor
6	magnetic	c	tape
7	binary	b	arithmetic
8	declaration	a	statement
9	comment	i	line
10	relational	d	operator

Language Focus D

Organizing information

Exercise 1 [p.50]

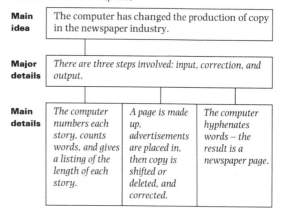

Main idea	The computer has changed the production of copy in the newspaper industry.
Major details	*There are three steps involved: input, correction, and output.*

Main details	*The computer numbers each story, counts words, and gives a listing of the length of each story.*	*A page is made up, advertisements are placed in, then copy is shifted or deleted, and corrected.*	*The computer hyphenates words – the result is a newspaper page.*

Exercise 2 [p. 51]

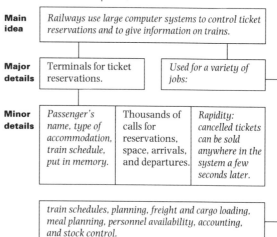

Main idea	*Railways use large computer systems to control ticket reservations and to give information on trains.*

Major details	Terminals for ticket reservations.	*Used for a variety of jobs:*

Minor details	*Passenger's name, type of accommodation, train schedule, put in memory.*	Thousands of calls for reservations, space, arrivals, and departures.	*Rapidity: cancelled tickets can be sold anywhere in the system a few seconds later.*

train schedules, planning, freight and cargo loading, meal planning, personnel availability, accounting, and stock control.

5

Computer software

Task 1 [p.52]

Suggestion 1 The teacher can ask individual students to make a list and to answer the questions in writing.

Suggestion 2 In pairs or in small groups, students can make a list and answer the questions. Then new pairs or groups can be formed and new information can be added to each student's notes. This can be repeated as often as necessary.

The teacher elicits information from the students and writes it on the board.

Extra information

Common PC-based software products include word processors, spreadsheets, desktop publishing software, and communications software.

Common word-processing and DTP features are listed in the tables on pages 58–59 of the Student's Book. Features of a word processor that might not be commonly used include: mail merge (a facility to generate mail shots from a mailing list), index (a facility to build an index automatically for a document), table of contents generation, and a thesaurus.

Task 2 [pp.52–53]

The teacher can ask students to read the opinions individually or in pairs and check which one corresponds to their own opinion.

Suggestion 1 Students read the text alone, then complete the opinion table provided.

Suggestion 2 In groups of four, students read the introduction silently, then each student reads about a different person. After reading about a person, each student tells the other three what he/she has read and they complete the opinion table together. If necessary, new groups of four can be formed and the activity repeated.

The teacher checks the answers at class level.

Answers

Opinions

	Mary Evans	Gerry Harper	Matt Andrews	Bob Bolton
In general, customers are getting what they want.	√			√
In general, customers are not getting what they want.		√	√	
Software is too complex.		√		
Software is not complex enough.				
Software developers know what users want.	√		√	
Software developers don't know what users want.				

Task 3 [p.54]

Alone, in pairs, or in groups of four, students decide which paraphrase is closest in meaning to the sentence from the text. At class level, students discuss their choices and reach a consensus.

Answers

1 a **2** b **3** a **4** b **5** b

Task 4 [p.54]

Suggestion 1 Nominated students can be asked to give their opinion to the class.

Suggestion 2 In small groups, students can discuss their choices and give reasons for them.

Task 5 [p.54]

Alone or in pairs, students can find the answers, check with another student or pair, and then check with the teacher.

Answers

1 cut through	**6** versatile
2 shifting	**7** overwhelming
3 prevail	**8** accomplish
4 purchasers	**9** exceed
5 read	**10** feedback

Task 6 [p.54]

Alone or in pairs, students translate the text and pass it on to another student or pair for editing. Then, the students get together to discuss the editing.

Students give their translations to the teacher for correction.

The teacher may wish to take the opportunity of discussing some of the problems and techniques of translation.

Task 7 [p.55]

Before playing the tape, the teacher should ensure that students know that Liz is female and Sam is male. The students should be given time to read the sentences carefully before they listen.

The teacher then plays the tape, and students decide whether the statements are true or false.

Later, in pairs, students discuss each statement and say why they think the information is true or false. Together they listen again and make the false statements into true statements. Then, new pairs can be formed and the activity can be repeated before the teacher elicits responses from each pair to check the answers.

Tapescript

BARRY HARRIS: Welcome to *Computer Forecast*. I'm Barry Harris and today's topic is the future of Software Technology. With me today are Sam Barton, representing the Software Manufacturers' Federation, and Liz Graham, a writer on *Business Computer Magazine*. Liz, Sam, welcome to the programme. We'd all agree that software technology is getting more complicated. Would you, the experts, characterize most PC software users as sophisticated, repeat buyers or first-time buyers? Liz Graham, can I start with you?

LIZ GRAHAM: No, I don't think that most PC users are sophisticated – far from it. Compared with users on other systems, they are far more tolerant of faulty design.

BARRY HARRIS: That's a very strong claim, Liz. Aren't you exaggerating the problem?

LIZ GRAHAM: No, I don't think I am exaggerating. I honestly think the vast majority of software users I've interviewed are not at all sophisticated. In fact, they're barely able to cope with the programs they're using. I estimate they probably use only ten per cent of the features in any given application. Now, we all agree that new software will definitely be bigger and much more complicated, so the problem can only get worse.

BARRY HARRIS: Sam, do you agree with Liz?

SAM BARTON: No, I think Liz isn't giving the whole picture. Maybe some single-users are inexperienced but, in a large company, I'd say that the buyers are definitely sophisticated and knowledgeable: they know what they're doing.

BARRY HARRIS: As a manufacturer, which represents your biggest market: the experienced buyer or the newcomer – the first-time buyer?

SAM BARTON: I think there are both sophisticated repeat buyers and first-time buyers who are buying PCs at the moment, just like always. In fact, I'd say it was about half and half. Of course, this makes it very tricky for a software developer, as the needs of the two groups are really quite different.

BARRY HARRIS: OK, the next thing I want to ask you all about is multimedia. Will multimedia have any serious effect on the software market? Liz?

LIZ GRAHAM: No, I don't think so. Maybe when the hardware price drops drastically, it'll be different, but I doubt it. Most users don't have access to the technology to make multimedia work for them. It takes more than a Mac or a Laser Writer to do multimedia.

BARRY HARRIS: What do you think, Sam?

SAM BARTON: I disagree with Liz again, I'm afraid. I really believe multimedia is having a serious effect on the market now. I feel it definitely has a future for things like presentations, visual effects, in fields like advertising or public relations. I'm convinced there will be a significant market for multimedia in the future, but it won't be as large as DTP.

BARRY HARRIS: We have time for one last question. Do you think developers are paying more attention to making software to be used with local area networks? Liz?

LIZ GRAHAM: Yes, I think they're doing so now. No serious application on the market today can exist without being network compatible.

BARRY HARRIS: Sam?

SAM BARTON: There's no question that we're paying more attention to LANs. New products that ignore the ability to adapt themselves to network use simply won't survive.

BARRY HARRIS: Well, I'm glad we've found at least one point on which both our guests can agree! That's all the time we have for today, I'm afraid. Liz, Sam, thank you very much for sharing your thoughts with us.

Answers

1 T
2 F (Liz thinks the users only *use* about ten per cent of the features on an application)
3 T
4 F ('I'd say it was about half and half')

5 T

6 T

7 F (Sam believes multimedia will have a significant market, but not as large as desktop publishing)

8 T

Task 8 [p.56]

Alone or in pairs, students try to fill in the missing words, then listen again to check that their answers are correct.

Answers

1	sophisticated	6	barely
2	faulty	7	estimate
3	claim	8	definitely
4	honestly	9	get
5	vast	10	worse

Task 9 [p.56]

In small groups, students discuss each question and take notes. Students then regroup and repeat the activity, adding more information to their notes. This can be repeated as many times as necessary.

Students should be the main contributors in this exercise but the teacher may wish to establish some areas for discussion.

Extra information

1 Software developers are inevitably seeking a new concept in general-purpose business software that, once developed, no one would be able to do without. Previous examples of this are word-processing packages and spreadsheets. Spreadsheets were an incredible breakthrough in end-user computing. It was the advent of spreadsheets which made everyone add more memory to their PCs in the 1980s.

2 Most educational software fails because it cannot easily adapt to the pace of the student and cannot adequately interact with the student in the way that a teacher can. If you could make educational software as absorbing as games software and teach at the same time, this would be ideal.

Comparing software packages

Task 10 [p.57]

Alone or in pairs, students try to match each feature with the correct definition. The teacher then checks at class level.

Answers

1	e	6	a
2	f	7	d
3	i	8	j
4	h	9	g
5	b	10	c

Task 11 [p.58]

Alone or in pairs, students try to fill in the gaps with the correct words.

The teacher then checks at class level.

Answers

1 Ami Pro 2.0/JustWrite

2 JustWrite

3 have all the features

4 Professional Write Plus/Word for Windows 2

5 Wordperfect for Windows/Wordstar for Windows

Task 12 [pp.58–59]

Alone or in pairs, students try to identify the products.

Students then check with the teacher at class level.

Answers

a Ami Pro for Windows 2.0

d PageMaker 4.0

b Legacy

e Ventura Publisher Windows 4.0

c PageMaker 3.01

Task 13 [p.59]

The teacher can remind students about paragraph structure (see Language focus D, page 49.)

Suggestion 1 Alone, students can write a paragraph and give it to the teacher for correction.

Suggestion 2 In pairs, students can discuss the content of their paragraph and collaborate in writing it. Then they can share their paragraph with another pair for editing purposes before giving it to the teacher for evaluation.

Extra information

Wordstar for Windows has all of the features compared but is one of the more expensive products, though less expensive than Word for Windows, which also has all of the features. However, Word is produced by Microsoft, which is the dominant force in the PC software market and thus will be compatible with more products. Most grammar checkers are not very good, and so JustWrite looks an attractive product in terms of price.

Task 14 [p.59]

The procedure is explained in the Student's book. The teacher can focus on the useful expressions and practise their pronunciation before the students start.

Task 15 [p.60]

Across

1 application
2 software
3 mailmerge
4 loop
5 spreadsheet
6 multimedia
7 linkage
8 publishing
9 developer
10 package

Down

11 compatible

Language Focus E

Making comparisons

Exercise 1 [p.64]

2 *superlative*: the most sophisticated
3 *equivalence*: similar
4 *non-equivalence*: faster than
5 *superlative*: One of the most important
6 *non-equivalence*: unlike

Exercise 2 [pp.64–65]

1 *non-equivalence*: better
2 *non-equivalence*: easier
3 *superlative*: user-friendliest
4 *non-equivalence*: not much bigger than
5 *superlative*: the closest
6 *equivalence*: both
7 *superlative*: best
8 *equivalence*: all
9 *non-equivalence*: superior to
10 *non-equivalence*: not in comparison to

6

Computer networks

Task 1 [p.66]

Suggestion 1 Alone or in pairs, students can answer the questions in writing.

Suggestion 2 The teacher can discuss the questions with the students at class level.

Answers

1 A local area network: this provides the ability for a group of computers to communicate directly within a relatively restricted area, usually within one building. It does not require the use of public telephone lines.

2 A wide area network: this provides the ability for computers to communicate over large distances using public telephone lines. These may be international. WANs may be used to connect up a number of LANs.

3 A distributed system is one in which the processing is spread over a number of computers connected by a network. The network is used to pass information and control the processes.

Task 2 [p.66]

Alone or in pairs, students try to match each word with the correct definition. They check with the teacher at class level.

Answers

1 c   2 b   3 d   4 f   5 a   6 e

Task 3 [p.67]

Suggestion 1 Alone, students read the text, then decide which statement is a summary of which paragraph.

Suggestion 2 In groups of five, each student reads only one paragraph. Then, each student takes turns telling the other students the information he/she has read. The group decides which statement (**a, b, c, d, e**) is a summary of the information they have just heard.

Finally, students check at class level with the teacher.

Answers

a 2   b 3   c 5   d 1   e 4

Task 4 [p.68]

Alone or in pairs, students fill in the gaps with the words provided. Students can check their answers with another pair or with the teacher.

Answers

1 protocols
2 distinction
3 distributed systems
4 workstations
5 screen handling
6 queries
7 parses
8 LANs
9 synchronous
10 fibre-optic
11 environments

Task 5 [p.68]

Alone or in pairs, students can complete this activity by referring back to the text for the correct word reference. Then, they can check their answers with another student or pair, or with the teacher.

Answers

1 blurred
2 locality
3 perform
4 price
5 global

Task 6 [p.68]

1 localized
2 cooperate
3 enabling
4 vast
5 reduce

Task 7 [p.69]

Suggestion 1 Alone, students translate the text and give their translations to the teacher for correction.

Suggestion 2 In pairs, students translate the text, then pass their efforts on to another pair for editing. Finally, the pairs get together to discuss the editing.

The teacher may wish to take the opportunity of discussing some of the problems and techniques of translation.

Task 8 [p.69]

Alone or in pairs, students predict whether the statements will be mentioned or not mentioned in the text. They then listen to the tape and check their predictions.

After checking their answers, students can compare answers in pairs or small groups. Finally, the teacher check answers at class level.

Tapescript

INTERVIEWER: Good afternoon, ladies and gentlemen. Welcome to *Computerworks*. Today's guest is Mary Marsh, a computer consultant and expert on networks and their applications. She'll be answering your questions on LANs. Mary, thanks for coming on the programme.

MARY MARSH: It's a pleasure, Mike.

INTERVIEWER: If you want to speak to Mary Marsh, the number to ring is 071-888 1200. The lines are now free. Mary, one of the impressions that business computer users have is that LANs are only for large businesses. Are they right?

MARY MARSH: Well, Mike, I don't agree that LANs are only for large companies. They're just as useful for smaller companies, as many of them are beginning to realize.

INTERVIEWER: Another common belief among business network users is that something as complex as a LAN can be designed and installed only by a specialist company. Is this correct?

MARY MARSH: No, I think they're wrong again, I'm afraid. It's perfectly possible for small companies to design and install their own LANs. Only the really big LANs for large companies need to be installed by outside experts.

INTERVIEWER: So, are you saying that every small company should install its own LAN – build a sort of do-it-yourself network?

MARY MARSH: No, not necessarily everyone. A great deal depends on your ability to work with computers and your willingness to spend time on LAN installation in addition to your normal work. Not everyone is capable of setting up a do-it-yourself network. If you don't have enough computer knowledge, or enough time, you

shouldn't attempt it. However, in some cases, you can do part of the installation work, even if you don't do the whole job yourself.

INTERVIEWER: Mary, let's go to our first caller, John from Leeds. Hello, John. What's your question, please?

1ST CALLER: Hello, Mary. My question is this: how much do you have to know about computers to install your own LAN?

MARY MARSH: Well, John, you certainly don't need a college qualification in computer science to do a simple LAN installation. On the other hand, you should be able to open up your machines and add and remove expansion boards easily. Also, you should be familiar with computer documentation. Are you used to doing all those things, John?

1ST CALLER: Yes, Mary, I've got quite a lot of experience.

MARY MARSH: Well, that's fine. Another point I'd want to make is that you have to be ready to try a process several times before you get it right.

INTERVIEWER: So, Mary's advice is that you've got to keep trying, John.

1ST CALLER: Yes. Thanks, Mary.

INTERVIEWER: OK, let's move on to our second caller, Alison from Sunderland. Hello, Alison, what's your question for Mary Marsh, please?

2ND CALLER: Hello, Mike. Hello, Mary. Mary, how much downtime should I expect while installing a LAN?

MARY MARSH: Hello, Alison. When you're installing a LAN, you may be without your computers for as much as a day or so. A lot depends on how well the installation proceeds, and *that* depends on your own experience. Professional installers can have each of your machines out of operation for only a few minutes at a time. If you can't live without your computers for a while, you might want to avoid doing it yourself.

INTERVIEWER: Does that answer your question, Alison?

2ND CALLER: Yes. Thank you very much, Mary.

INTERVIEWER: Let's go to caller number three, Bill from Bristol. Hello, Bill. What's your question for Mary?

3RD CALLER: Hello, Mary. I'd like to know if I have to be good at construction techniques to install a LAN?

MARY MARSH: Well, Bill, installing a LAN involves running cable to several offices. This may require you to install junction boxes in walls, do the wiring, and maybe install electrical power as well. If you aren't familiar with these skills, and if you aren't a qualified electrician, you will need to hire someone for this part, at least. Of course, if you're installing your LAN in one room, then you might not need to hire anyone.

3RD CALLER: That's what I thought. Thank you very much.

INTERVIEWER: OK, I'll be back with my guest, Mary Marsh, answering questions about computer networks, right after this break . . .

Answers

1	☑	5	☒
2	☑	6	☑
3	☒	7	☑
4	☒	8	☒

Task 9 [p.70]

Alone or in pairs, students can try to fill in the gaps with the missing words. Then, they can listen to the text a second time to check their answers. Students can discuss other possibilities with the teacher.

Answers

1	without	7	offices
2	well	8	power
3	experience	9	familiar
4	out	10	qualified
5	operation	11	anyone
6	avoid		

Network configurations

Task 10 [pp.70–71]

Alone, students can read the texts and match each illustration with a text.

Students check their answers with the teacher.

Answers

1 b   2 d   3 a   4 c

Task 11 [p.72]

Alone or in pairs, students can write the questions to the answers provided. Each student can then share his/her questions with another student, then go through it with the teacher.

Answers

1 What is the central switch used for?
2 Can data move in more than one direction?
3 Can more than one device send information at any moment?
4 How do devices know that the message is for them?
5 What happens when a sending device detects another's transmission?

Task 12 [p.72]

Alone or in pairs or groups of three, students decide which network configuration the flowchart refers to and check with the teacher, giving their reasons.

Extra information

This network configuration refers to the Bus/Ethernet network configuration. Each diamond represents a decision and each rectangle a process. Starting in the top left hand corner, the network device listens to see if anyone else is sending. Following this, it makes a decision based on what is happening. If there is no one else and if there is data to send, a transmission takes place and the network device then listens again to see if there was a collision.

Task 13 [p.72]

Alone or in pairs, students try to match the characteristics with the proper configuration. Students then work with another student or pair to discuss how they reached their decision. They then check with the teacher and discuss their strategies.

Answers

a Bus/Ethernet: this has a varied time response depending on the other traffic on the network and the number of collisions going on. It is easy to expand because devices may just be plugged in, or in the case of thick wire Ethernet, clamped on to the cable. If a device on the work fails, it does not usually bring the whole network down. It is simple because the network conceptually consists of one piece of cable terminated at each end.

b Ring: because a device can only transmit when it has control of a token which is transmitted at fixed intervals, the response time is predictable. Reconfiguration requires breaking the network to add new devices. Any device failing on the network can bring the whole network down as it will fail to forward the tokens. Because of the above reasons and wiring considerations, bus networks are more complex to install and administer.

Task 14 [pp.72–73]

The teacher can present the students with useful language and revise question forms, practising pronunciation and stress before students begin the task.

Suggestion 1 As explained in the Student's Book.

Suggestion 2 Repeat the activity with the students exchanging roles.

Extra information

Netplan Eazy is a low-budget, entry-level network for between two and six PC users. This will allow users to share data, software (licences permitting), and printing facilities. In addition, e-mail software is provided with the network, allowing fast and easy communications between users. The network can be installed by anyone just using a screwdriver. The entry-level kit costs £215 for the first two users and £100 for each user after that.

Task 15 [p.74]

Across	Down
1 user interface	2 synchronous
5 install	3 area network
7 broadcast	4 expansion
9 local	6 WAN
10 switched	8 star

Language focus F

Time sequence

Exercise 1 [p.76]

<u>During</u> the seventeenth and eighteenth centuries, many easy ways of calculating were devised. Logarithm tables, calculus, and the basis for the modern slide rule were invented <u>during</u> this period. It was not <u>until</u> the early 1800s that the first calculating machine appeared and, <u>not too long after</u>, Charles Babbage designed a machine which became the basis for building <u>today's</u> computers. A hundred years <u>later</u>, the first analog computer was built, but the first digital computer was not completed <u>until</u> 1944. <u>Since</u> then, computers have gone through four generations: digital computers using vacuum tubes <u>in</u> the 1950s, transistors <u>in</u> the early 1960s, integrated circuits <u>in</u> the mid-60s, and a single chip <u>in</u> the 1970s. <u>In</u> the 1980s, we saw computers become smaller, faster, and cheaper. <u>Earlier</u> this decade, computers became portable, from laptops to palmtops. At the rate computer technology is growing <u>now</u>, we can expect further dramatic developments <u>before</u> the end of the century.

Exercise 2 [p.77]

2 *during*: Over
3 *after*: later
4 *before*: ago
5 *after*: When
6 *before*: for the last ... years
7 *after*: Eventually
8 *before*: Until

Exercise 3 [p.77]

1 Traditionally (1. 6): *before*
2 now (1. 16): *during*
3 Originally (1. 20): *before*
4 Today (1.23): *during*
5 In the 1980s (1.65): *before*
6 During the early part (1.68): *before*
7 Since (1. 75): *after*
8 At the same time (1.89): *during*

Computer viruses

Task 1 [p.78]

Alone or in pairs, students can write answers to the questions.

The students can discuss these at class level with the teacher.

Answers

1 A computer virus is an unwanted program that has entered your system without you knowing about it. Viruses are often hidden on computer disks inside a file containing a legitimate program so that they are not easy to detect without special tools. They are often spread by the sharing of games or other disks, although viruses have also been found on disks sold by reputable software manufacturers.
2 It may damage, alter, or interfere with the normal running of your computer, or it can be harmless but irritating, affecting only the screen.

Task 2 [p.78]

Alone or in pairs, students try to match each word with the correct definition.

Answers

1 c	3 h	5 b	7 a
2 f	4 e	6 g	8 d

Task 3 [p.79]

Suggestion 1 Alone, students read the text, then in pairs compare the information in the text with their answers to Task 1.

Suggestion 2 Treat this as an interactive reading task, following the procedure described in Suggestion 2, Task 5 (Unit 2), on page 6.

Students then compare the information in the text with their answers to Task 1.

Task 4 [p.80]

Alone or in pairs, students decide whether the statements are true or false. They then make the necessary changes to the false statements.

Answers

1 F
2 F
3 F (it is the detonator which does this)
4 F (the text says that Lehigh damages the data on your disk)
5 F (the text says many, not most)
6 F
7 F (the text doesn't mention how many there are, but there are now thousands in existence)
8 F (the text doesn't say this and, in fact, the two have different purposes)

Task 5 [p.80]

Alone or in pairs, students can complete this activity by referring back to the text for the correct line reference. Then they can check their answers with another student or with the teacher.

Answers

1 79
2 148–149
3 18–19
4 130–135

Task 6 [p.80]

Alone or in pairs, students can write the questions to the answers. Each student or pair can then share their questions with another student.

Example answers

1 How many parts does a virus have?
2 How does the detonator work?
3 When is the Lehigh detonator triggered?
4 How often does the virus infect?
5 Can you keep your computer free of viruses?

Task 7 [p.80]

Alone or in pairs, students can complete this activity by referring back to the text for the correct word reference. Then they can check their answers with another student or pair, or with the teacher.

Answers

1 the infector and the detonator
2 a computer virus
3 COMMAND.COM
4 the Lehigh infector
5 that file
6 Many viruses have spread . . .
7 virus shields
8 viruses

Task 8 [p.81]

1 replicates	6 enlarging
2 spread to	7 installed in
3 altering	8 erases
4 instantly	9 aware
5 grumble	10 rarely

Computer security

Task 9 [p.81]

In pairs or groups, the students discuss the questions. Students regroup several times and take notes every time they get new information.

The students then discuss the questions at class level with the teacher.

Extra information

1 The original meaning of the term 'hacker' was someone who enjoys exploring the details of computer systems and how to stretch their capabilities, as opposed to most users who prefer to learn the minimum necessary. Obsessive programmers were called hackers. In recent years, this term has begun to be used to refer to people who try to breach other people's computer security to gain illegal access.

2 Security in a computer can be improved in a number of ways:

- requiring passwords or a physical device like a magnetic card to access the computer at all
- requiring passwords to access data once a person is in the computer system
- validating passwords to ensure they are not commonly used words

- ensuring that all users have their own IDs and that there are no unallocated IDs
- not allowing any dial-in access to the system or, if there is dial-in access, ensuring that the modems have a dial-back facility to confirm that the user is calling from a known and authorized location
- having PCs/workstations without floppy disk drive so that users cannot introduce viruses
- having virus detection software installed on every PC

Task 10 [p.81]

Alone or in pairs, students read the questions before listening.

Suggestion 1 Alone, students listen to the tape and try to answer the questions. They may have to listen a second time to complete their answers.

Suggestion 2 Alone, students take notes while they listen, then, together with one or two other students, compare their notes and add the information that is missing.

Students check their answers with the teacher, listening again to the appropriate parts of the tape.

Tapescript

RICHARD: Hi, Steve. Are you busy?

STEVE: No, not really.

RICHARD: Good. If you've got a minute, I'd like to talk to you about computer security. I saw a program on TV the other evening about computer hackers. It made me realize that our network system isn't very secure. We have a lot of sensitive information in our data bank, and I think perhaps we should install some kind of system to protect it.

STEVE: That's a good point. Theoretically, anyone could call in and connect their personal computers at home to the office network. All they'd need is a modem.

RICHARD: Exactly. There's nothing to stop students calling in and changing their grades, for example. They could even change their records to show that they'd paid for a course when they hadn't.

STEVE: Hmm. What we need is a password.

RICHARD: Yes, but the problem with passwords is what people do with them. Some put them on scraps of paper on their computer terminals. Others use their own names, or a partner's name. That just makes life easy for a hacker.

STEVE: True, but it's not just what people do with them. The whole idea of using real words is risky. There are programs now that will try every word in the dictionary. If you want to make life difficult for the hackers, it's much safer to use a random mixture of numbers and letter.

RICHARD: I suppose so. But isn't it possible to buy a security system?

STEVE: Of course. It depends how much you want to spend. You can even buy a system that changes the password every single minute.

RICHARD: Every minute? Then how do the authorized users know what the password is?

STEVE: They carry a smart card that shows a constantly changing number. The number is the password.

RICHARD: Very clever!

STEVE: Yes, as long as you don't leave your card lying around.

Answers

1 The network system isn't very secure.
2 A modem.
3 What people do with them, e.g. use their own name or a partner's name, which makes life easy for a hacker.
4 It shows a constantly changing number. It is safe as long as you don't leave the card lying around.
5 Steve seems to know a lot, but see Extra information 2, Task 9, on page 27 for advice he did not mention.

Task 11 [p.82]

As explained in the Student's Book. The teacher may give students useful language for giving advice before they begin this activity.

Task 12 [pp.82–83]

Alone or in pairs, students can try to match each item in the list with a corresponding letter in the flowchart. Then, they can share their information with other students or the teacher.

Answers

a 4   b 5   c 2   d 6   e 7   f 1   g 3

Task 13 [p.83]

Alone or in pairs, students can complete this activity by referring back to the text for the correct word reference. Then, they can check their answers with another student or pair or with the teacher.

With weaker classes, teachers may decide to help students by giving paragraph references for each of the words or phrases.

Answers

1 evil
2 lurks
3 wreaking havoc
4 meddlers
5 strike fear into the hearts of
6 teams
7 spotted
8 scary
9 options
10 invaders

Task 14 [p.83]

In pairs or in small groups, students can discuss each question and take notes for possible answers. Regroup students as often as necessary in order for each student to get as much information as possible. The teacher may conduct a discussion at class level.

Example answers

1 The advertisement is trying to frighten the would-be purchaser with worries about unauthorized access to a PC and the possible threat of viruses. These concerns are valid. The advertisement goes on to try to assure the purchaser that their product can cure all the problems outlined in the advertisement.
2 Although the advertisement does point this out, the product is only for stand-alone PCs. Today many PCs are connected to networks and this can be the source of danger. A virus loose on a network could destroy the entire network. A virus on a stand-alone PC is a nuisance, but provided one has taken adequate backups, it is not a disaster. The advertisement also fails to explain technically how it recognizes unknown viruses.
3 More technical information, and testimonials from other major corporate users.

Task 15 [p.84]

Suggestion 1 Alone, each student can design an advertisement before giving it to the teacher for correction.

Suggestion 2 In pairs or groups, students can discuss the content of their advertisement and collaborate in writing it. Then they can share their final product with another team for editing purposes before giving it to the teacher for evaluation.

The teacher can circulate providing help and advice.

Task 16 [p.84]

Alone, students can read and answer the questions in writing. Then, they can discuss their answers in small groups, and with the teacher at class level.

Extra information

A worm is a type of computer virus that spreads on a network of computers. The effect of a worm may vary, but it can cause a lot of damage and sufficiently disrupt a network so that it no longer functions. This is apparently what happened in the case quoted in the newspaper article. The cost of removing the worm and cleaning up the damaged data in the 6,000 institutions would have been considerable in man-hours alone.

Task 17 [p.85]

protective	destructive
signature	detonator
write-protect tab	infect
password	hacker
cipher	infector
smart card	erase
keyboard lock	worm
virus scanner	pirated
shield	
access control	

Students provide their own classifications.

Language focus G

Listing

In both the exercises below, answers other than those given are possible.

Exercise 1 [p.87]

1 first
2 then
3 Thirdly
4 Next
5 Another
6 next
7 Finally

Exercise 2 [p.87]

1 first
2 next
3 Then
4 Also
5 then
6 The next
7 Lastly

8

Computers in the office

Task 1 [p.88]

Alone or in pairs, students can identify the pictures and make a list of any other examples of computer technology that are used in the office. Then, they can share their information with other students in the class, regrouping if necessary, or discussing with the teacher at class level.

Answers

a multimedia on screen
b OCR (optical character recognition) scanner
c radiation screen
d pen-based/clipboard computer

Task 2 [pp.88–89]

Suggestion 1 Alone, students read the text, then check their lists to see how many items were mentioned in the text.

Suggestion 2 Treat this as an interactive reading task, following the procedure described in Suggestion 2, Task 5 (Unit 2), on page 6.

The teacher can check their answers at class level.

Answers

These will obviously vary from student to student. The aspects of computer technology mentioned in the text are as follows:

radiation screens (l. 1), e-mail (l. 21), OCR/DIP (document-image-processing) (l. 29), pen-based computing (p. 38), multimedia (l. 52), CD-ROM (l. 60), portable computers (l. 65), FAX boards (l. 75), voice recognition (l. 81), large display screens (l. 116), colour (l. 124), wrist rests (l. 138), networks (l. 144).

Task 3 [p.90]

Alone or in pairs, students can complete the table by making notes from the text. Then, using their notes, they can share their information with another student or pair, adding and/or deleting information as they see fit.

Make sure that student are aware that there is room for only ten items in the table (approximately one per paragraph). This means that some items need to be grouped together – e.g. e-mail/OCR/DIP, all of which allow you to accomplish electronically what you would normally do with paper. However, items need not be grouped exactly as below.

Information in brackets is not in the text.

Answers

Item	Current/potential use
radiation screens	protect user from harmful emissions
e-mail/OCR/DIP	allow you to accomplish electronically what you would normally do with paper
pen-based computer	in its infancy (but used for form-filling and drawing)
multimedia	presentations and training
CD-ROM	storing/accessing large amounts of information
portable computers	(computing while travelling), getting smaller
voice recognition	in its infancy but verbal interaction with computer will be possible
large display screens/colour	reduced eye strain
wrist-rests/keyboard design	fewer repetitive-strain injuries
networks	data access and world-wide communications

Task 4 [pp.90–91]

Alone, or in pairs or groups, students can decide which paraphrase is closest in meaning to the sentence from the text.

Students then check their decisions with the teacher and discuss the reasons for their choices.

Answers

1 a   **2 a**   **3 b**   **4 b**

Task 5 [p.91]

Alone or in pairs, students complete this activity,

then check with another student, pair, or the teacher for the correct answer.

Answers

1d (there are few colloquialisms, but the style is almost conversational in places)

2a (it is very dense; it is full of references to technologies and products which would be difficult for a general reader to comprehend fully)

3c (because of the spelling of certain words, e.g. *color*)

Task 6 [p.91]

Alone or in pairs, students can complete this activity by referring back to the text for the correct word reference. Then they can check their answers with another student or with the teacher.

Answers

1 Radiation screens
2 the battle
3 the other half
4 the technology
5 Voice recognition
6 Speaking to your computer
7 the traditional keyboard
8 Internet

Task 7 [pp.91–92]

Alone or in pairs, students can complete this activity by referring back to the text for the correct word reference. Then they can check their answers with another student or with the teacher.

Answers

1	entire	9	safety
2	normally	10	create
3	valid	11	plentiful
4	appear	12	combine
5	credible	13	major
6	reducing	14	upwards of
7	proliferating	15	suffering
8	ripe	16	alleviate

Task 8 [pp.92–93]

Alone or in pairs, students find the answers, then check with the teacher.

Answers

1a *consider*   **2a** *applicants*
  b *considerable*   **b** *applicable*
  c *consideration*   **c** *applying*
  d *considerably*   **d** *applications*

3a *explanatory*   **4a** *dependably*
  b *explanation*   **b** *dependence*
  c *explain*   **c** *dependable*
  d *explained*   **d** *depend*

5a *connectivity*
  b *connections*
  c *connector*
  d *connected*

Task 9 [p.93]

Suggestion 1 Alone, students read the steps, then listen to the tape and put the steps in the right order. They may have to listen a second time to complete this activity.

Suggestion 2 Alone or in pairs, students first try to order the steps by predicting. They then listen to the tape to check their answers.

Finally, the teacher checks arrives at class level.

Tapescript

DAVID: So tell me, Charles, how have you applied document-image-processing technology at your company? What exactly happens in the process?

CHARLES: Well, David, first of all, when a document arrives in the mailroom, the envelope is opened by a machine. Then, its pages are removed and arranged by a clerk. Next, these pages are transferred to a mail analyst.

DAVID: What is the analyst's job?

CHARLES: He or she reads the mail to determine the applicable customer and the routing of the document. This information is then entered into the computer.

DAVID: Does the analyst have to supply routing and indexing data?

CHARLES: No, that's largely automated. All the analyst needs to do is enter two items: an IMS index transaction, which is a descriptive code often composed of the form number, and then the customer name. The computer supplies the routing and indexing data.

DAVID: What happens once the index is stored?

CHARLES: Once the index is stored, a temporary key number is generated and written on the document.

DAVID: How much time does all that take?

CHARLES: Believe it or not, only 11 seconds. That's all the time it takes for this step.

DAVID: That's pretty fast! So, after the document's scanned, what's the next step?

CHARLES: The last phase of the input process involves checking the quality of the scan and entering the temporary document ID number to link it with the index that's already been generated.

DAVID: How soon can it be available on the system?

CHARLES: Once the document number's entered, any user in the system can access the document, including users at remote sites.

DAVID: How long does it take to retrieve a document?

CHARLES: If the document's been processed within the past year, it only takes 15 or 20 seconds. Requests for older documents take longer because an operator must manually mount an archived disk.

DAVID: Well, your system sounds quite impressive. What kind of advantages are we taking about? Money, time?

CHARLES: Actually both. We've saved 39,000 square feet of office space and freed 120 employes from file maintenance. The net saving is approximately three million pounds per year.

DAVID: Well, it sounds like the move to DIP has certainly been a success here. I wonder if . . .

Answers

1	h	5	e	9	c
2	j	6	a	10	l
3	b	7	k	11	f
4	g	8	i	12	d

Task 10 [p.94]

Alone or in pairs, students answers the questions, then compare their answers with another student or check with the teacher.

Answers

1a 11 seconds.
 b 15/20 seconds.
2 The operator must mount an archived disk manually.
3a 39,000.
 b 120.
 c three million.

Task 11 [p.94]

Suggestion 1 In small groups, students discuss the questions and jot down information.

Suggestion 2 In pairs, students discuss and draw up a list of negative aspects. Then, each student forms a group with three other students, and the activity is repeated in order to generate more information.

Extra information

Benefits: computers can be used to save costs, either by increasing existing human efficiency, or by saving on the number of staff required to perform certain tasks. Networks of computers can, if used correctly, improve human communications (however, relying on computers for communication runs the risk of losing some vital human interaction). Some businesses would not have grown to their current sizes without computers to aid them. Producing thousands of invoices per day without a computer is a daunting task.

Negative aspects: the disadvantages of replacing people with computers in the office are that the people you retain need a higher skill level. The lesser-skilled people become unemployed, and there are fewer jobs for unskilled people. The office becomes dependent on technology and, if it breaks down, the office can no longer function effectively. It can take longer to train newcomers to the office to become effective in their day-to-day jobs.

Task 12 [p.94]

Alone, students can scan all the information in the unit and draw up a list of benefits and negative aspects. Then, they can compare their information with another student, regrouping if necessary, to repeat the activity in order to get as much information as possible.

Suggestion 1 Alone, students can produce their paragraphs, then share them with a classmate for editing purposes before giving them to the teacher for evaluation.

Suggestion 2 In pairs, students can produce their paragraphs, then share them with another pair for editing purposes before giving them to the teacher for evaluation.

The teacher may wish to offer a checklist of contents and guidelines for text organization.

Information systems

Task 13 [p.94]

The teacher asks students to choose the best definition, alone or in pairs, and discusses their opinions at class level.

Answers

a is the closest definition.

Task 14 [pp.94–95]

Alone, the students can predict whether the statements are true or false, then discuss their predictions with a partner.

Suggestion 1 Alone, students can read the text, then check their true/false predictions.

Suggestion 2 Treat this as an interactive reading task, following the procedure described in Suggestion 2, Task 5, (Unit 2), on page 6.

The students check their answers with the teacher, looking back also at their answers to Task 13 in the light of the opinions expressed in the text.

Answers

1 F   2 F   3 T   4 T   5 T

Task 15 [p.95]

Suggestion 1 Alone, students can draw the diagram required.

Suggestion 2 In pairs, students discuss the information in the text and collaborate on the drawing of the diagram.

Answers

The information in the text can be expressed in many different ways. What is important is the configuration of the diagram (i.e. how the various parts interrelate) rather than the layout on the page.

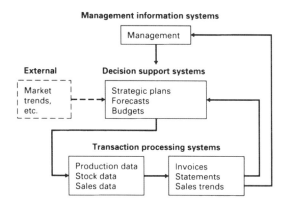

Task 16 [p.95]

Suggestion 1 Alone, students write a paragraph based on their diagram. Then, they can share their paragraph with another student for editing purposes before comparing it with the original text or giving it to the teacher for evaluation.

Suggestion 2 In pairs, using one diagram, students collaborate on writing a paragraph. They then share their paragraph with another pair for editing purposes before comparing it with the original or giving it to the teacher for evaluation.

Task 17 [p.96]

Across

1 information
2 monitor
3 processing
4 converter
5 display

6 support
7 recognition
8 transaction
9 digitized

Down

10 footprint

Language focus H

The passive

Exercise 1 [p.97]

1 are registered
2 is evaluated
3 is allocated
4 is required

5 is contacted
6 is arranged
7 are dealt with
8 be supplied

Exercise 2 [p.98]

1 is called
2 is used
3 are passed on
4 is stored

5 are transformed
6 are performed
7 is opened
8 is stored/is generated/ is written

Exercise 3 [pp.98–99]

1 was founded
2 was developed
3 were made
4 were sold

5 were set up
6 was built
7 were launched
8 was reversed/was taken

9

Computers in education

Task 1 [p.100]

Alone or in pairs, students make their lists.

Extra information

Computers are used in education in the following technologies: CD-ROM, interactive video, computer-assisted learning, multimedia, distance learning (where student and tutor connect their computers via modems and telephone lines), etc.

Task 2 [p.100]

Students discuss the questions in groups of three or four. The teacher rounds up at class level.

Answers

1 Computers could be used to teach such courses as CAD/CAM, programming, writing, mathematics, languages, etc. The class can discuss which courses they (or friends) are taking using computers, and how they are used. There may be computers available for students to use on their own, in the library or in a media centre. Many libraries have computerized catalogues. Students may also mention how computers are used by the administration. You may encourage this part of the discussion or limit it to examples of technology used in learning itself.

2 a Further education is also called continuing education, adult education, extension classes, etc. It involves the continuation of the education process after a student has left the normal school system.

   b Open learning means learning that is open to everyone, irrespective of age, qualifications, background, etc. Courses offered therefore tend to be at a fairly basic level.

   c Flexible learning means learning tailored to fit the needs of learners. It includes day release courses (in which companies allow employees one day off for study per week), evening classes, and distance learning.

Task 3 [pp.100–101]

Alone, students read the text to find the information, underlining the answers as they find them. They then compare their answers with those of another student. The teacher checks around the class and takes this opportunity to discuss the skill of skimming/scanning (i.e. reading quickly through a text to find specific information).

Answers

1 To bring beneficial change to the processes of learning in education and training, through the development and application of educational technology.

2 Learning technology.

3 They design and produce learning materials in all subjects to support education and training.

4 NCETs Schooling Directorate is pursuing four priorities.

5 Women, older workers, and those who use information technology to work from home.

6 Satellites, CD-ROM, and interactive video.

Task 4 [p.102]

Alone or in pairs, students do this exercise. The teacher should encourage them to use their own words by finding synonyms or equivalent expressions to those used in the text, and by summarizing portions of the original text. The teacher checks the results with the class, discussing the appropriateness of different answers.

Inform students that, in most cases, they will need to write more than one line to answer the questions properly.

Example answers

You It covers many areas, including the use of computers, satellites, and interactive video in education and industry, and issues of copyright and flexible learning.

You We design and produce varied learning materials. We do research, project management, technical consultation, and training. We also provide expertise in many areas of education and an information service.

You Yes. We run a programme to help teachers apply I.T. in schools.

You We do work with children and young adults, as well as the handicapped.

You The Training Directorate is in charge of programmes aimed at those who wish to continue their learning after school-leaving age.

You Yes, it does. We have worked on language training and Artifical Intelligence Systems.

You It follows the latest technological developments and maintains a national expertise on standards and requirements.

Task 5 [p.102]

Students work in pairs or small groups to make the list. Students explain to the teachers what each of the terms means, giving a definition or an example.

Answer

satellites, CD-ROM, interactive video, desktop publishing, remote sensing (a technology involving the use of satellite armed with powerful infra-red cameras, which photograph geographical and man-made features on Earth), teleconferencing systems, audio-visual systems

Task 6 [p.102]

Alone or in pairs, students find the answers. The teacher checks at class level.

1	embraces	5	handicapped
2	benefits	6	run-up
3	comprehensive	7	abreast
4	curriculum	8	watching brief

Task 7 [p.102]

Suggestion 1 Alone, students translate the text.

Suggestion 2 In pairs, students translate the text, then pass it on to another pair for editing. Finally, the pairs get together to discuss the editing.

Students give their translations to the teacher for correction.

The teacher may take this opportunity to discuss translation problems and techniques.

Task 8 [p.103]

Students take notes and prepare their presentation in pairs or small groups. The teacher makes certain that they are not simply copying out entire sections of the text. The goal of this exercise is for students to find the main ideas in a text and summarize them. During the presentations, the students who are listening can take notes and then check to see if the presentation was complete. These presentations could also be taped to provide a basis for reviewing the content. The teacher should check that the students not only include the main points in the text, but that they are also able to express them in their own words.

CALL

Task 9 [p.103]

Alone or in pairs, students decide whether the statements are true or false by predicting, using their own knowledge of the subject. The teacher then plays the tape, and students check their predictions against what they hear.

Alone or in pairs, students make the necessary changes to the false statements.

Then, with another student or pair, the activity can be repeated before the teacher elicits responses from students to check the answers at class level.

Answers

1 T
2 F (you should check that there is good applications software available)
3 F (not two factors but three factors, the third being the size of your budget)
4 T
5 F (the ideal is one computer per student and all computers linked by a local area network)
6 F (free access = unlimited access)

Task 10 [p.104]

Alone or in pairs, students try to fill in the missing word. The teacher then plays the last part of the recording while students check their answers.

The students then check with the teacher at class level.

Tapescript

TEACHER 1: Tony, I'm sorry to begin with an obvious question, but, em, what exactly is CALL?

TONY LONGSTONE: CALL stands for Computer Assisted Language Learning. In fact, CALL is a very general term which is used to describe the use of computers in any form as part of a language course.

TEACHER 1: When you say 'in any form', do you mean that *all* uses of computers in language education can be described as CALL?

TONY LONGSTONE: Well, yes, within reason. Obviously, if a teacher is using a computer just to type out a worksheet, or if a private college provides a computerized bill for a student for language course fees, that doesn't count as CALL. The computer has to be actively used by the students as well.

TEACHER 2: What sort of computer do you need?

TONY LONGSTONE: Well, an important thing to find out at the beginning is what software is available for the machine or operating system you're thinking of buying. If there's no available software specifically written for CALL, you should check that there is at least some good applications software available, such as word processing, databases, and spreadsheets.

TEACHER 2: Mm. How many machines do you need?

TONY LONGSTONE: That depends very much on factors like the number of students, the amount of space available, and, above all, the size of your budget. In an ideal world, you would have one computer per student, and all the computers would be linked by a local area network. This would allow the students to exchange material and send each other information and messages.

TEACHER 1: But supposing we can't afford that level of investment. Is it possible to have CALL using only one computer?

TONY LONGSTONE: Yes, provided that you organize things properly.

TEACHER 1: Mm. Could you be more specific?

TONY LONGSTONE: Well, if you are going to have just one computer available, you should try to get a screen that's big enough for all your students to see. Alternatively, you could use a display device which will allow you to project the picture from the computer on to an overhead projector.

TEACHER 2: Talking about organization, what's the best way to organize the equipment, in your opinion?

TONY LONGSTONE: Again, that depends on your situation. I think the most common way of organizing computers is to locate them in one special-purpose computer room, with the furniture set out so as to allow group work at machines. However, if you prefer to limit your CALL activities to one computer per class, the ideal would be to have one computer permanently in each of your classrooms. If this isn't possible, a good solution is to install the equipment on a trolley which can be taken into the classroom for the lesson. Of course, computers needn't be limited to the classroom.

TEACHER 1: What do you mean?

TONY LONGSTONE: Well, given sufficient resources, it's a good idea to have some computers available for teachers in the teachers' room. Also, it's very useful to have a self-access facility for use by students. In both cases, they – eh, teachers and students – can gain a lot of confidence and proficiency by having free access to the equipment. Finally, an excellent idea is to have one computer with a large screen functioning as an electronic noticeboard for messages prepared for students and staff. This should be located in a public part of the instutition, such as the hall or library. I first saw this system used in a school in . . .

Answers

1	resources	5	equipment
2	available	6	noticeboard
3	facility	7	library
4	proficiency		

Task 11 [p.104]

Suggestion 1 Students individually prepare their answers and then discuss them in groups of four.

Suggestion 2 The teacher starts the discussion at class level to get some ideas going. Students then form groups of four and continue the discussion.

Example answers

1 Advantages: software often provides instant feedback; students can learn at their own pace; students can control their progress; computers don't get tired; content can be customized to suit particular needs; gaining computer literacy is a desirable skill in today's world.

Disadvantages: can be impersonal; some students (and teachers) have difficulty adapting to machines; computers cannot answer all the student's questions, etc.

2 The answer is probably 'no' because computers are unlikely to be able to provide the same interaction as a human being can in terms of variety of responses, feedback on points that are not included in the software package, etc. A teacher will probably know more about language and how it is used than the programmed software available for computers. Teachers can intervene at any time to help students with any problem, no matter when it comes up. If anyone answers 'yes', make certain his/her choice is supported by valid reasons.

Task 12 [pp.104–105]

Alone or in pairs, students can fill in the notes. They can then find another student or form groups of three to compare their answers. The teacher checks at class level, focusing on the principles of note-taking, such as cutting out or making the minimum necessary use of auxiliaries, articles, pronouns, etc.

Answers

1 course book/reader/newspaper
2 analyse/level of difficulty/compare/syllabus
3 created *or* generated/printed worksheets/screen
4 knowledge/menu/five/manual
5 twenty-five/files/password/access

Task 13 [p.106]

Alone or in pairs, students can find the answers, then check with another student and with the teacher.

Answers

1 **a** *creation*   **b** *creating*   **c** *creativity*
2 **a** *generated* **b** *generation* **c** *generate*
3 **a** *access*   **b** *access*   **c** *accessible*
4 **a** *analysed*   **b** *analysis*   **c** *analyses*

Task 14 [p.106]

Suggestion 1 Students work individually, and then, in pairs, compare their reports.

Suggestion 2 In pairs, students write their reports.

Students may have to listen to the tape several times to get enough ideas to write a report. The first paragraph of your students' reports will probably be quite similar. The second paragraph will vary, depending on the elements individual students, or pairs, decide to include, and how much detail they obtain from listening to the conversation. The third paragraph will vary widely, since it depends on the content of the second paragraph and students may choose any of the elements to support their recommendation.

Example report

First of all, the letters CALL stand for Computer Assisted Language Learning. This term is applied to any use of computers in a language course where students are actively using the computer.

There are different options available for using computers in a language class. The ideal set-up is to have one computer for each student and then to have all the computers linked up by a local area network so that students can exchange information and messages. Another option is to have a special computer room with a number of networked PCs that are available for students to work on. If this is not possible, one computer could be installed in each classroom. If only one

computer is available, there must be a way of showing what is on the screen to all the students at the same time, using either a large-screen computer monitor or a display device on an overhead projector.

For our institute, I would recommended a special computer room, I realize we do not have enough money to buy a computer for every student, but having only one computer in a classroom would make it difficult to give individual students time to work on it. Our teachers are interested in using computers with their students, and I feel that a special room would provide a centre for encouraging students and teachers to master their new technology.

Task 15 [p.107]

1 access
2 teleconferencing
3 remote
4 database
5 analyse
6 vocational
7 interactive
8 terminal
9 spreadsheet

Hidden word satellite

Language Focus I

Giving examples

Exercise 1 [p.108]

computer – mainframe, microcomputer, PC
input device – trackball, stylus, mouse
output device – printer, VDU
programming language – APL, COBOL, C
network configuration – bus, star, ring

Example sentences

There are many different possibilities.
1 Several types of computers are available, depending on your needs. For example, there are mainframes, microcomputers, and PCs.
2 Many people find input devices such as a trackball, a stylus, or a mouse are easier to use than the keyboard.
3 A printer and a VDU are illustrations of an output device.
4 Students study many programming languages, including APL, COBOL, and C.

Exercise 2 [p.109]

Marker		Main idea
2	including	clipboard computers
3	e.g.	a special language
4	an example	a simple virus
5	such as	a PC that has public access

Exercise 3 [p.109]

Main idea	Examples
microchip technology	computers, washing-machines, cars, books . . . as part of public databases, networks of computers

10

Computers and medicine

Task 1 [p.110]

Suggestion 1 The teacher can ask individual students for their ideas and make a list on the board.

Suggestion 2 In pairs or in small groups, students can discuss their ideas and make a list. Then, new pairs or groups can be formed and new applications can be added to each student's list. This can be repeated as often as necessary. Afterwards, the teacher can elicit information from the students and write it on the board.

Try to find examples in magazines or newspaper articles to show your students, or have students bring them to class.

Example answers

Various types of implants such as pacemakers, monitoring equipment, scanning equipment, laser technology, surgery, communicating for handicapped people or people with impaired abilities, etc.

Task 2 [pp.110–112]

Make sure the students can describe each of the cards in English. Ask the students to find relationships between the various cards. Elicit ideas from the students and write all the ideas generated on the board, even the strangest ones. Students then read the text to find the answers and discuss them with the teacher at class level.

Answers

1 The message is to a male aphasic patient's wife. The cards mean: 'Go to the grocery store and buy some poultry'.
2 Students may provide a variety of answers. In fact, the four cards were used because the hypothetical person giving the message has a problem formulating his thoughts into coherent sentences.
3 A computer could help to convey messages like this by providing a bank of pictures which a person could select to make up 'sentences' like the one in the picture, simply by moving a computer mouse.

Task 3 [p.112]

Students read the text and then, alone or in pairs, decide on the most suitable answer for the text. The teacher discusses their ideas at class level.

Once you have talked about the three titles suggested, you could ask your students to think up other titles and have them justify their choice of words. Encourage creativity. Give your comments on their choices.

Answer

Students will probably disagree on the best title. **2** is the worst, because it contains no true information about the text: computers are not cable of caring. In fact, **1** was the original title, but that does not necessarily mean it is the best.

Task 4 [pp.112–113]

Alone, in pairs, or in groups of three, students complete the text with appropriate words. They then check their answers at class level. Answers other than those given below may also be correct.

Answers

1 dependent
2 communicate
3 guess
4 capable
5 developed
6 lack
7 damaged
8 awkward/time-consuming/cumbersome
9 increased
10 improved/transformed

Task 5 [p.113]

Alone, or in pairs or small groups, students decide on which paraphrase is closest in meaning to the sentence from the text.

At class level, students discuss their choices and reach a consensus.

Answers

1 b   2 a   3 a   4 b

Task 6 [p.113]

Alone or in pairs, students can find the answers, then check their answers with another student or pair and then with the teacher.

Answers

1 h	3 i	5 a	7 b	9 f
2 e	4 j	6 c	8 g	10 d

Task 7 [p.114]

Students can work on this task in class, or prepare the exercise for homework.

Task 8 [p.114]

Procedure is explained in the Student's Book. For this task, be sure students only read the text that has been assigned to them. The teacher can go around and listen to the various pairs, making a note of those who have clear summaries. Some students can then give their summaries to the entire class once all the pairs have finished their work.

Data storage and management

Task 9 [p.115]

The students read through all the questions alone or in pairs, predicting the content of the listening extract. The teacher may need to focus on new vocabulary.

Suggestion 1 Alone, students listen to the tape and try to answer the questions. They may have to listen a second time to complete their answers.

Suggestion 2 Alone, students take notes while they listen, then together with two other students, compare their notes and add the information that is missing.

Students check their answers with the teacher, listening again to the appropriate parts of the tape.

Tapescript

INTERVIEWER: What size is the database at Grovemount Hospital?

ALEX COLLINS: Pretty big! To give you some idea: over a five-day period of care for one patient, somewhere in the region of 25,000 characters of data might be generated. That would include matters relating to the patient's medical history, laboratory reports, medical treatment, invoices,

and so on. Now, if we have an average of, say, 300 occupied beds, that means well in excess of 500 million characters of stored data per year.

INTERVIEWER: And that is presumably only data relating to patients?

ALEX COLLINS: Precisely. We also have data relating to the administration of the hospital – em, for example, information on staff, bed occupancy, that sort of thing.

INTERVIEWER: So how exactly is the database organized?

ALEX COLLINS: Well, our database is organized in the same way that any other database is organized. The basic component is a named collection of data called a file. The file called PATIENT, for example, contains the name, address, date of birth, National Health Service number, etc. of each patient. Within each file there is a collection of records of the same type. So, in the case of the patient file, each record relates to a single patient. Each record must obviously have a unique identifier so that it can be accessed in the database.

INTERVIEWER: You mean a name or number?

ALEX COLLINS: Yes, usually a combination of the two.

INTERVIEWER: Right. So each file contains an organized collection of records. Does that mean that each individual record has an internal structure, too?

ALEX COLLINS: No, not necessarily. I've already said that all records in a given file must be of the same type. Well, all the patient records *do* have an internal structure – or fixed format, as we call it. This means that each component – name, date of birth, etc. – is stored separately and can be accessed separately. However, some files contain free-format records, and in those cases each record simply contains a long string of text.

INTERVIEWER: You mean letters, reports, that kind of thing?

ALEX COLLINS: Yes.

INTERVIEWER: I see. Now, can you tell us what happens when the database is updated?

ALEX COLLINS: Yes. Each input message is called a transaction. When a transaction enters the system for processing, the computer must retrieve related data from the database. At the end of the processing, the computer stores updated data to reflect the changes caused by the transaction.

INTERVIEWER: Could you give an example?

ALEX COLLINS: Yes, of course. Each time a patient is admitted to the hospital, the database must be updated to show his or her details. This is obvious. However, the database must also be updated to show that there is one less bed available. This will, in turn, affect summary operational data, such as bed occupancy for the month, and so on.

INTERVIEWER: OK. But you have lots of different people accessing the database at the same time, don't you?

ALEX COLLINS: It's a multi-access system, yes.

INTERVIEWER: Right. But what happens if two people access the same data at exactly the same time?

ALEX COLLINS: Hm. It can't happen. In that situation, the database management system would grant access to one of the users only. The other user would have to wait until the first transaction was processed and the data updated.

Answers

1 c   2 a   3 b   4 c   5 b

Task 10 [p.116]

Alone or in pairs, students read the extract and fill in the gaps.

Suggestion 1 The teacher plays the relevant section of the tapescript, and students check their answers.

Suggestion 2 The teacher asks students for their answers and writes them all (whether right or wrong) on the board. The students may change their minds at this stage. The teacher then plays the tape and students check their answers. The teacher should point out any answers which are appropriate, even if they are not those actually used in the recording.

Answers

1	updated	7	operational
2	input	8	occupancy
3	message	9	multi-access
4	retrieve	10	exactly
5	transaction	11	grant
6	available	12	users

Tasks 11 [p.116]

Alone or in pairs, students match the definitions. They then check with the teacher at class level.

Answers

1	f	3	a	5	b
2	d	4	e	6	c

Task 12 [pp.116–117]

In pairs or small groups, students answer the questions and build up a list on the blackboard with the teacher. Then they read the text and compare their answers with it. The teacher discusses their answers at class level.

Answers

1 The text mentions details about patients, X-rays, and scans. Databases can also be used for inventory control, patient details, billing rates, treatment details, treatment statistics, drug records, bed records, staff records, etc.

2 A database management system.

3 Its function is to manage multi-user databases – to handle requests for access to data from users, manage record locking for multi-user access, provide users with their own views of the data, provide database integrity recovery in the event of system failure, and split data structures from the program accessing the data (very important for systems maintenance, as it allows the data structure to be easily changed without necessarily having to modify all programs accessing the data).

Task 13 [p.117]

Alone, or in pairs or small groups, students put the steps in the correct order and check with the teacher at class level.

Answers

Correct order: **4, 2, 3, 6, 1, 5**.

Task 14 [p.118]

The students work in pairs following the instructions in the Student's Book. The teacher may allow students to make short notes before beginning the activity. The teacher should then go around and listen to the various pairs, discussing any problems at class level when they have finished.

Example answers

Student A: A DBMS is a system that allows many users to have access to a database and get different kinds of information from it. The DBMS makes data stored in a database available and intelligible to the person who has asked for information. It transforms the data from machine code to something the user can understand. It allows users to ask a question in 'normal language' in order to get information from data stored in 'computer language'.

Student B: A user makes an access request using a language that the DBMS understands. The DBMS then inspects various schema. Next the various application programmes perform the required operations on the data that is stored in the databases. The DBMS then constructs a logical view of the data that was asked for by the user.

Task 15 [pp.118–119]

Students work individually and then check with another student or with the teacher at class level.

Answers

Across

1 virtual
2 external
3 schema
4 internal
5 instrument
6 image
7 machine code
8 in-batch
9 multi-user
10 compressing
11 reality

Down

12 transmitter.

Language Focus J

Explanations and definitions

Exercise 1 [p.121]

1 term: *input*
   group: *information*
   characteristics: *presented to the computer*
2 term: *computer*
   group: *parts of hardware*
   characteristics: *in which calculations and other data manipulations are performed*
   (term: *computer*)
   group: *high-speed internal memory*
   characteristics: *in which data and calculations are stored during actual executions of programs*
3 term: *system*
   group: *integrated parts*
   characteristics: *working together to form a useful whole*
4 term: *large computer systems*
   group: *computer systems*
   characteristics: *found in computer installations processing immense amounts of data*

Exercise 2 [pp.121–122]

1 term: *control unit*
   group: *part of the processor*
   characteristics: *which controls data transfers between the various input and output devices*

2 term: *modem*
   group: *device*
   characteristics: *which serves a dual purpose*
3 term: *compiler*
   group: *systems program*
   characteristics: *which may be written in any language*
   term: *compiler's operating system*
   group: *true systems program*
   characteristics: *which controls the central processing unit, the input, the output, and the secondary memory devices*
4 term: *variable*
   group: *quantity*
   characteristics: *that is referred to by name*
5 term: *WAN*
   group: *network*
   characteristics: *connected over long-distance telephone lines*
6 term: *LAN*
   group: *localized network*
   characteristics: *usually in one building or in a group of buildings close together*
7 term: *computer virus*
   group: *unwanted program*
   characteristics: *that has entered your system without you knowing about it*
8 term: *virus shields*
   group: *antivirus programs*
   characteristics: *which detect viruses as they are infecting your PC*
   term: *virus scanners*
   group: *antivirus programs*
   characteristics: *which detect viruses once they've infected you*

11

Robotics

Task 1 [p.123]

Alone, in pairs, or in small groups of three or four, students decide on the functions and then tell the class their ideas.

Extra information

a A robot for shearing sheep.

b An insect robot, designed using ideas derived from a branch of artificial intelligence known as 'artificial stupidity'. The robot is capable of going into places that normal robots cannot go (because of size) to check welds, etc. The robot shown is actually a prototype.

c A typical robot arm used in the car industry. It can be programmed to do a number of repetitive tasks.

Task 2 [p.124]

Before the students start listening to the tape, either the teacher or the students read out each of the events, checking that the vocabulary is understood.

Play the tape once and ask the students to match the events with the correct year. Play the tape again if students are having problems. In pairs or small groups, students compare their answers and then check with the teacher at class level.

Tapescript

Welcome to the National Science Museum's new exhibition: *Robots: past, present, and future*. This recording is intended to guide you through our exhibits. Before we begin our tour, let's briefly review the history of robots in the twentieth century. Of course, you could argue that the history of robots goes back way before our own century. Throughout history, people have tried to invent machines to perform a whole variety of tasks, such as writing, drawing, or even playing musical instruments.

The word 'robot' was invented by the Czech playwright, Karel Čapek. It comes from the Czech word for 'work'. In Čapek's play *RUR* (*Rossum's Universal Robots*), which came to London in 1921, the robots became so intelligent and so disillusioned with their human masters that they revolted. They destroyed the humans and created a new world inhabited only by robots. This theme of ungrateful robots rebelling against their human creators is one that has been used by many science fiction writers.

In 1954, the American inventor George Devol began work that eventually led to the industrial robot as we know it today. His company, the Unimation Company, developed flexible industrial machines and began to market them in the early sixties. Since then, many companies have entered the robotics market.

Between 1967 and 1969, researchers at the Stanford Research Institute in the United States developed a robot with wheels named Shakey. Shakey was fitted with bump detectors, a sonar range finder, and a TV camera. All three helped Shakey to move freely and avoid obstacles. However, at the time, Shakey was thought to be a failure. This was because it could only be controlled by a separate mainframe computer, which sent its commands to the robot through a radio channel.

The next important step was the development of robots with legs. In 1967, the General Electric Corporation (GEC) had developed a four-wheeled machine for the US Department of Defense. The machine carried a human operator who had to control each of the four legs. This was an extremely difficult job for the driver, and the machine regularly became unbalanced and fell over.

Later devices were more successful – for example, a four-legged robot developed at the Tokyo Institute of Technology in 1980. This system combined a human controller with automatic processing of information about the terrain, right down to the foot movements needed to ensure smooth movement.

In 1983, a six-legged robot was developed by Odetics Incorporated, for commercial production. A battery-powered model, Odex I, used a radio channel for leg control and a video link for conveying images. This machine could walk over obstacles and lift loads several times its own weight.

Meanwhile, research continues on machines that rely on one or two legs. In 1984, Marc Raibert developed one-legged hopping robots at Carnegie-Mellon University in the USA.

Now, let's begin our tour of the exhibits. As you enter room 1, you can see on your left one of the earliest . . .

Answers

1 c	3 f	5 b	7 d
2 e	4 a	6 g	

Task 3 [p.124]

Alone or in pairs, students try to decide whether the statements are true or false before the tape is played for the second time. The teacher then plays the tape, and students check their answers against what they hear. Alone or in pairs, students make the necessary changes to the false statements. Then, the teacher elicits responses from students to check the answers at class level.

Answers

1 F (the history of robotics goes back way before our own century)
2 F (in Čapek's play, *RUR*, the robots become so intelligent and disillusioned with their human masters that they destroy them)
3 T
4 T
5 F (all Shakey's movements were controlled by a separate mainframe computer)
6 T
7 F
8 T

Task 4 [pp.124–125]

Suggestion 1 In pairs, students brainstorm ideas about which jobs are suitable for humans or robots, and why. They fill in the table with their ideas. One student can act as secretary for the discussion.

Suggestion 2 The class brainstorms with the teacher who makes notes on the board. The students copy the lists into their books.

The students then read the text and compare their ideas with the author's. The teacher can conduct a class discussion when they have finished.

Extra information

Robots are not good at any job which requires unusual dexterity and which is not repetitive, e.g. washing a baby, styling a person's hair, etc.

Task 5 [p.126]

Alone or in pairs, students can complete the table by making notes from the text. Then, using their notes, they can share their information with another student or pair, adding and/or deleting information as they see fit. They then check at class level.

Answers

Job or environment	Reason
Welding	machine are heavy and hard to handle for humans
Carrying components, etc.	will not harm or put stress on robots
Spray painting	robots are not affected by poisonous fumes
Assembling components	requires extreme accuracy; robots can be programmed to repeat actions without error
In nuclear reactors, underwater, etc.	robots can work in conditions which are either dangerous or impossible for human beings

Task 6 [p.126]

Alone or in pairs, students can write the questions to the answers. Each student can then share his/her questions with another student, and then go through the exercise with the teacher.

Example answers

1 How much does a welding tool weigh?
2 Why is automatic accuracy valuable in the electronics industry?
3 In what kind of projects are robots equipped with video cameras and other sensing devices used?
4 What are researchers doing to expand the range of robotic applications?
5 Can robots be compared to nature's handiwork?
6 According to some industrialists, what will all their employees be doing by the year 2000?

Task 7 [p.126]

In pairs, students complete this task. The teacher should check that they follow the principles of note-taking.

Answers

	1	2	3
Animal	snake	elephant	octopus
Aspect	vertebrae	trunk	tentacles
Reason	to move in many directions	to lift heavy objects	to hold fragile objects with gentle pressure

Task 8 [p.126]

Alone or in pairs, students can complete this activity by referring back to the text for the correct word references. Then, they can check their answers, with other students or with the teacher.

Answers

1	handle	5	imitate
2	fixing	6	simulated
3	costly	7	fragile
4	expand	8	accelerates

Task 9 [p.127]

Suggestion 1 Alone, students translate the text.

Suggestion 2 In pairs, students translate the text, then pass it on to another pair for editing. Finally, the pairs get together to discuss the editing.

Students give their translations to the teacher for correction.

Task 10 [p.127]

Suggestion 1 In small groups, students discuss each question and take notes.

Suggestion 2 As Suggestion 1 except that students regroup and repeat the activity adding more information to their notes. This can be repeated as many times as necessary.

The teacher rounds up at class level.

Extra information

1 Students may not agree with robots being companions in the home or soldiers in the armed forces, or with other applications, depending on their personal views of the future. When they do disagree, they should justify their opinions. If they do not disagree, they should give some concrete examples of how they think specific applications would be used.

2 Some implications might be: less work to do, more interesting work for people, new social values (no work ethic), changing roles of family members, and robots taking control.

Robot characteristics

Task 11 [p.128]

Alone or in pairs, students read the text and do the matching exercise. The teacher checks at class level.

Answers

1	b	2	c	3	a	4	e	5	d

1	Cyborg	4	Flexible machine
2	Android	5	Automaton
3	Mobile robot		

(1 = the most similar to humans; 5 = the simplest)

Task 12 [pp.128–129]

Before students attempt this exercise, the teacher should check that they understand all the words given at the end of the text. Alone or in pairs, students can fill in the gaps with the appropriate words. They can check their answers with each other and with the teacher.

Answers

1	closed-loop	5	proportional
2	grasp	6	attached
3	compares	7	converts
4	direction		

Tasks 13 [p.129]

Students will be able to put their creative skills to use in this exercise. Make certain they understand what the terms 'pitch', 'yaw', and 'roll' mean. In pairs, students design a robotic hand, paying attention to include the three degrees of rotational freedom illustrated. They then find another pair and take it in turns to explain and comment on their inventions.

Task 14 [p.129]

Alone, or preferably in their original pairs from Task 13, students label their invention and write a description of it. (The teacher can remind students of the language studied in Language focus J on page 120.)

Give the students help if they don't know what to call the various parts of their invention. Once the paragraphs have been written, this task could be linked to the previous one. Selected students could show the drawings of their inventions, and read out their descriptions, to see if the other students can follow the explanations. Students could ask questions for clarification if parts or procedures are not clear to them.

Example diagram

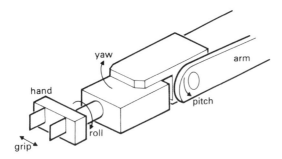

Task 15 [p.130]

2 briefcase: the rest are classes of portable computer
3 monitor: the rest are parts of the central processing unit of a computer
4 drive: the rest are types of magnetic disk
5 assembler: the rest are high-level languages
6 loop: the rest are network configurations
7 sentry: the rest are types of robot
8 virtual: the rest are database terms

Language focus K

Compound nouns

Exercise 1 [p.132]

Point out to your students that in this form of compound, the descriptive noun usually reverts to the *singular* form. For exampe, in 'computer programming', computer is singular.

Answers

1 a visual display unit
2 a magnetic card reader
3 a graph plotter
4 a laser printer
5 a magnetic disk holder
6 a ink jet printer
7 a date transmission rate
8 a multimedia presentation package
9 a batch processing program
10 a computer disk conversion process.

Exercise 2 [pp.132–133]

When students are doing this exercise, they will have to put some nouns back into the *plural* for the purposes of their explanation. For example, number **2**, 'an optical character reader' reads characters.

Example answers

1 a device that inputs information
2 a device that reads optical characters
3 a stylus for creating graphics
4 a program that sorts documents
5 a system for the transmission of fibre optics
6 a register for the control of sequences
7 a device that displays using liquid crystals
8 information for the configuration of a network
9 a program for managing documents on top of your desk
10 a software package/a package of software for editing multimedia

12

Virtual reality

Task 1 [p.134]

In pairs or in small groups, students discuss the question and make a list. Students may have played video games which make use of this technology. The teacher rounds up ideas at class level, checking vocabulary and pronunciation.

Extra information

Examples of virtual reality, some of which are found in the text, include: controlling a robot without previous programming, going through a building before it is built, using a device before it is made, travelling in space before you get there, learning to drive a car before you get on the road, using sign language to make a computer speak, special effects in movies, recreating scenes from the past. In short, virtual reality makes it possible to experience doing something without really doing it.

Task 2 [pp.134–135]

Suggestion 1 Alone, students read the text, then in pairs compare the information in the text with their answers to Task 1.

Suggestion 2 Treat this as an interactive reading task, following the procedure described in Suggestion 2, Task 5 (Unit 2), page 6.

The teacher rounds up at class level.

Task 3 [p.136]

Alone or in pairs, students can complete the activity. The teacher checks the answers at class level, asking students to identify the exact reference in the text.

Answers

1 The term comes from the mathematical concept of an image that has the virtues of a real object without the substance.
2 Britain leads the world in VR research.
3 When robots are controlled by mounted video

cameras, there is a time lag between seeing the image and sending a corrective control signal.
4 With Robert Stone's system, a user can 'feel' objects because the data glove has air pockets that are inflated to give a sensation of touch.
5 Video games will probably be the first major market for VR applications.

Task 4 [p.136]

Alone or in pairs, students can complete this activity by referring back to the text for the correct word or phrase reference. Then, they can check their answers with another student or pair, or with the teacher.

Answers

1 an illusion
2 virtual reality
3 divers
4 guiding a robot by looking at a picture from a video camera mounted on it and twiddling the controls
5 The helmet
6 what the wearer should be seeing in that direction
7 the object
8 a nuclear power plant

Task 5 [p.136]

Alone or in pairs, students can complete this activity by referring back to the text for the correct word or phrase reference. They then check their answers with another student or pair, and finally with the teacher.

Answers

1	at will	6	pads
2	virtues	7	inflated
3	fortunes	8	launched
4	plunge	9	mimic
5	twiddling	10	fighter

Task 6 [p.136]

Alone or in pairs, students can find the answers, then check with another student or pair and the teacher.

Answers

1a	*corrective*	**2a**	*detectable*	**3a**	*sensor*
b	*correctness*	**b**	*detect*	**b**	*sensitive*
c	*correctly*	**c**	*detection*	**c**	*sensation*

Task 7 [p.137]

Students will come up with various versions of this paragraph. The new paragraph should contain all the information contained in both the original paragraphs, without duplicating any of it.

In the example paragraph which follows, elements of the second paragraph have been incorporated in the first. Such elements are shown in italics.

Example paragraph

A virtual reality system consists of a helmet with a *liquid-crystal* colour display in front of each eye, and wide-angle lenses to cover the entire field of view and give a stereoscopic *image*. The helmet contains *a set of magnetic* sensors, rather like electronic compasses, to record where it is pointing *as it moves*. A computer calculates what the wearer should be seeing in that direction and displays it on the screen.

Task 8 [p.137]

Suggestion 1 Individual students read out each of the three responses and the students have a discussion at class level.

Suggestion 2 Give students a few minutes to think over their individual positions. You may want to encourage them to write down a few ideas before the discussion begins. Once you feel that everyone has formed an opinion, divide the students into small groups so they can discuss the three opinions and their own points of view. After the discussion, at class level, see if the students have changed their original opinions about the influence of virtual reality in computer war games on young people's attitude to violence.

Task 9 [p.138]

Alone, students write their paragraphs and give them to the teacher for correction.

The paragraphs will vary depending on each student's point of view. Students should start their paragraphs by discussing their reaction to the three responses in the book. Then they should give their own opinions on the subject.

The teacher can focus on useful language for expressing opinions in writing, such as *In my opinion. . ., I feel. . ., I believe. . ., I think. . .,* etc,

Task 10 [p.138]

Alone or in pairs, students read the questions before listening. The teacher should check that they understand the information required.

Suggestion 1 Alone, students listen to the tape and try to answer the questions.

Suggestion 2 Alone, students take notes while they listen, then together with two other students, compare their notes and add the information that is missing.

Students check their answers with the teacher, listening again to the appropriate parts of the tape.

Tapescript

INTERVIEWER: I'm here at the Virtual Reality Exhibition at Olympia in London. With me is Michael Emsley, who is one of the exhibitors. Michael, there's obviously an enormous amount of interest in VR. Do you think it can live up to people's expectations.

MICHAEL EMSLEY: That's a very good question. I think most people do expect far more from VR than it can give them – at least for the present, and this is largely due to the way the media have presented it.

INTERVIEWER: So what should people expect from it?

MICHAEL EMSLEY: Well, they shouldn't expect to be able to have a holiday abroad without leaving their living room, which is what quite a number of visitors today seem to think. VR should be seen as a means, not an end.

INTERVIEWER: What exactly do you mean by that?

MICHAEL EMSLEY: I mean that it should be seen as an 'enabling technology'. The potential applications are as diverse as robot operation in contaminated nuclear power stations, em, recreating crime scenes for the police, em, helping people with physical disabilities, and curing psychological problems.

INTERVIEWER: In other words, the ultimate interface between humans and computers?

MICHAEL EMSLEY: Potentially, yes.

INTERVIEWER: How long do we have to wait for these possibilities to become realities?

MICHAEL EMSLEY: Another good question, but difficult to answer. One thing is certain, though. If VR doesn't start producing results soon, then it is likely to run into the same problems as artificial intelligence.

INTERVIEWER: Meaning?

MICHAEL EMSLEY: Meaning that if there are no results soon, industry will stop investing in it. Then it certainly won't fulfil its potential.

INTERVIEWER: So, where is the technology at the moment?

MICHAEL EMSLEY: Well, the virtual worlds we can create today are still a long way from resembling the real world. This is mainly because of the visual system. Even the best VR display gives only a fraction of the detail of human vision.

INTERVIEWER: How is the display created?

MICHAEL EMSLEY: Most VR vision systems are headsets that block out everything except two liquid crystal display screens, one for each eye. Using a technique learnt from artificial intelligence work on vision, the images on each screen are distorted and displaced, giving the illusion of a three-dimensional view.

INTERVIEWER: What happens when the person moves his head?

MICHAEL EMSLEY: The movements are detected by three electromagnetic coils – one coil for movements up and down, one for left and right, and one for movements forwards and backwards. This information is digitized and passed to the computer, which then updates the data it holds on the popsition of the headset. Once the new position of the headset has been calculated, the visual display is updated.

INTERVIEWER: It sounds like a long process.

MICHAEL EMSLEY: It's only a matter of milliseconds, but there is still enough of a delay to be noticed by the person wearing the headset.

INTERVIEWER: How much computing power is needed to operate a VR system?

MICHAEL EMSLEY: (laughs) Even an unsophisticated visual system needs a processor able to handle about one hundred and twenty megaflops. To make what I would call a reasonable visual system would require a processor able to handle a thousand megaflops – and that's expensive!

Example answers

1 People expect so much from VR because of the way the media have presented it.
2 Michael Emsley thinks that VR should be seen as an enabling technology.
3 Two potential applications are (choose from these four):
   a robot operation in contaminated nuclear power stations.
   b recreating crime scenes for the police.
   c helping people with physical disabilities.
   d curing psychological problems.
4 If VR technology does not produce results soon, industry will stop investing in it.

5 The best VR system only gives a fraction of the detail of human vision.
6 There are three electromagnetic coils to control the three types of movement: up and down, left and right, and forwards and backwards.
7 It takes only a few milliseconds for the computer to calculate each new position of the headset and update the display.
8 To make a 'reasonable' visual system would take a computer able to handle a thousand megaflops.

Task 11 [p.138]

Alone or in pairs, students try to fill in the missing words. The teacher then plays the relevant section of the tape while the students check their answers. The teacher then checks answers at class level.

Answers

1	display	12	up
2	headsets	13	down
3	liquid	14	left
4	crystal	15	right
5	display	16	forwards
6	artificial	17	backwards
7	intelligence	18	digitized
8	distorted	19	updates
9	three	20	calculated
10	dimensional	21	process
11	electromagnetic		

VR input devices

Task 12 [p.139]

Students read the text quickly for general sense and then, in pairs, small groups, or at class level, discuss their ideas. The teacher elicits from the students what they feel the contradiction is, and discusses this at class level.

Example answer

The text contradicts much of what the newspaper article said about the hand input device. The newspaper article is very positive, while this text is largely negative.

There are (at least) two possible explanations for this contradiction:

1 The newspaper article may be deliberately trying to create a positive image of the technology (in order to make it more striking and exciting for the non-expert reader) by not mentioning any drawbacks.
2 The second text could be referring to an earlier version of the VR glove.

Task 13 [pp.139–140]

Alone or in pairs, students can complete the table, then check their answers with each other and with the teacher.

Problem of hand input device	Consequences
1 Same delays that affect the head mount display system.	User over-compensates, affecting interaction between hand and objects.
2 Limited ability to generate tactile feedback.	Any fine manipulation is impossible.
3 User's hand and arm are unsupported.	User has to work harder in VR than in reality; extended activity impossible.

Task 14 [p.140]

Alone or in pairs, students look for the words in the text and decide if their meanings are similar or opposite, then check their answers with other students or with the teacher.

Answers

1 S	3 S	5 O	7 S
2 S	4 S	6 S	8 O

Task 15 [p.141]

Across	**Down**
1 mathematical	1 manufacturing
6 lens	2 helmet
7 fine	3 manipulation
9 LCD	4 calculate
10 robotics	5 liquid crystal
11 glove	8 compass
12 virtual	

Language focus L

Classifying

Exercise 1 [pp.143–144]

1	control unit	14	Secondary memory
2	arithmetic-logic		
3	control unit	15	sequential
4	register	16	tape
5	decoder	17	random access
6	counter	18	disk
7	clock	19	input
8	arithmetic-logic unit	20	tape drive
9	registers	21	disk drive
10	binary adder	22	terminal
11	circuitry	23	output
12	primary memory	24	printer
13	secondary memory	25	terminal

Exercise 2 [p.144]

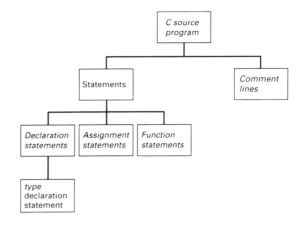

13

Machine translation

Task 1 [p.145]

Alone or in pairs, students can go through the statements. They should be encouraged to share any knowledge of MT systems. This can be extended to a class level discussion of the sentences.

Task 2 [pp.145–146]

Alone, students read the text, then, in pairs, they compare the information in the text with their answers to Task 1.

Answers

1 F   2 T   3 F

Task 3 [p.147]

Suggestion 1 Alone or in pairs, students re-read the text, match each paragraph to the correct summary, and identify the extra summary.

Suggestion 2 Treat as an interactive reading task, following the procedure described in Suggestion 2, Task 5 (Unit 2), on page 6.

Students then check their answers with the teacher.

Answers

1	6	6	2
2	4	7	not in text
3	8	8	1
4	3	9	9
5	7	10	5

Task 4 [p.147]

Alone or in pairs, students complete this task, referring back to the text in order to choose the correct synonymous expression. They then check their answers with another student or with the teacher.

Answers

1 d   2 f   3 b   4 a   5 c   6 e

Task 5 [p.147]

Students continue as in Task 4, this time finding the word or phrase in the text, checking with the teacher when they have finished.

Answers

1 laughable
2 glossies
3 blithely
4 bound to
5 bunch
6 black art
7 dabbling their toes
8 gone in at the deep end

Task 6 [p.147]

Students should be given a short time to think about this individually or in pairs, but the task should be discussed with the teacher at class level.

Answers

The problem lies in the word *set*, which is used in the example sentences as:

- a noun meaning 'group'
- a transitive verb
- part of the expression *to have one's hair set*
- an intransitive verb
- part of the phrasal verb *set off*
- part of a compound noun

Students could look for other vocabulary items that have many meanings. Here is another example.

Is there any *paper* in the box? I have a *paper* to write for my French course. We're going to *paper* the bedroom. You must show your *papers* at the customs office. I put last week's *papers* in the bin. Have you read the *papers* today?

Your students can probably come up with a lot more examples (*put, get, light, run,* etc.). Divide them into small groups and see which one can find the word with the highest number of different interpretations.

AI and expert systems

Task 7 [p.148]

In pairs or in small groups, students work together to come up with a definition for these two terms. They then listen to the conversation and make the necessary modifications to arrive at final definitions, which should be similar to those given below.

Make sure that students know to listen only for the definitions required. They should ignore all other information at this stage.

Answers

1 'Artifical intelligence' describes computer programs that perform tasks which require intelligence when done by humans.
2 'Expert systems' refers to programs written using the techniques of AI, which attempt to capture the knowledge of one or more experts in a particular topic. In addition to giving expert advice, they are designed to explain their 'reasoning'.

Task 8 [p.148]

Students read the questions through before listening. After listening, they can discuss their answers in pairs or in small groups. The teacher may play the tape again if necessary, and checks answers at class level.

The teacher may decide to pre-teach some of the terminology used (from the glossary). This is a difficult passage.

Tapescript

KEVIN: David, the last time we talked about AI, you said it was concerned with developing computer programs that perform tasks which require intelligence when done by humans.

DAVID: Yes, exactly.

KEVIN: OK. But then you gave some examples – playing games, understanding natural language, forming plans, er ... proving theorems. You also gave the example of visual perception. Now surely visual perception – seeing – doesn't require intelligence?

DAVID: (laughs) It may not seem so, Kevin, but perceptual tasks such as seeing and hearing involve a lot more computation than is apparent. But because this computation is unconscious in humans, it's much harder to simulate.

KEVIN: So you're saying that AI is better at intellectual tasks such as game playing and proving theorems than at perceptual tasks like seeing and hearing.

DAVID: I'm saying AI has been more successful at intellectual tasks.

KEVIN: Right, but in any case, AI is trying to simulate human behaviour.

DAVID: That's an oversimplification. Sometimes programs are intended to simulate human behaviour, as in computational psychology, but sometimes they're simply built for technological application, as in the case of expert systems.

KEVIN: Expert systems are part of AI, right?

DAVID: Well, to be more accurate, expert systems are programs built using the programming techniques of AI, especially techniques built for problem-solving. The actual subdiscipline of AI concerned with building expert systems is called 'knowledge engineering'.

KEVIN: What are expert systems used for?

DAVID: They're built for commercial applications. Up to now they've been used for a variety of tasks – medical diagnosis, electronic fault-finding, machine translation, and so on. But the point about them is that you can interrogate them about how they came to a particular conclusion.

KEVIN: So, in that respect, they imitate human experts.

DAVID: Yes. I read recently about a Japanese system that can be used by lawyers to draw conclusions about new legal cases. It refers to databases of statutory laws and legal precedents and is able to see similarities in the reasoning processes used to decide each case – exactly as a skilled lawyer would.

KEVIN: How can it do that?

DAVID: The system has two reasoning mechanisms, known as inference engines, which work in parallel. One operates on the written laws, the other operates on the legal precedents. They draw all the possible conclusions and then output them in the form of inference trees.

KEVIN: Inference trees?

DAVID: Yes. Inference trees show how each conclusion was arrived at. And that is what makes this program different from any normal program.

Answers

1 Yes, visual perception requires intelligence when done by humans, although it is done unconsciously.
2 The two categories of perceptual tasks mentioned are intellectual and perceptual.
3 AI is more successful at intellectual tasks.
4 Expert systems use AI programming techniques.
5 Examples of existing expert systems are medical diagnosis, electronic fault-finding, and machine translation.
6 Expert systems are like human experts because

you can question them about how they came to a particular conclusion.

7 The Japanese system has one to operate on the written laws, and one to operate on the legal precedents.
8 Inference trees show how each conclusion was reached.

Task 9 [pp.148–149]

Alone or in pairs, students try to predict the missing words. The teacher then plays the relevant section of the tape while students check their answers. Finally, in pairs, students can compare their answers before the teacher checks them at class level.

Answers

1	expert	9	reasoning
2	systems	10	skilled
3	applications	11	inference
4	diagnosis	12	engines
5	interrogate	13	parallel
6	conclusion	14	inference
7	lawyers	15	trees
8	databases		

Task 10 [p.149]

Alone, students read the text quickly (set a maximum time limit) to find the answers. Explain that they do not need to understand every word at this point.

Students then check with the teacher at class level.

Answers

1 ROI assists in the management of franchised retail operations. It creates work schedules, recommends marketing tactics, and helps with personnel hiring.
2 Scott French 'cloned' Jacqueline Susann by writing part of a book in collaboration with a computer using an AI program created to imitate the novelist.
3 Other applications of AI mentioned in the text are planning your garden, treating critically injured patients in emergency rooms, and using natural language front-ends in multimedia systems.

Task 11 [p.150]

Alone or in pairs, students complete this task by reading the text more carefully. The teacher checks the answers at class level.

Answers

1 ROI stands for Retail Operations Intelligence.
2 Burger King is developing an expert system to try to outperform its competitor, McDonald's.
3 Susann wrote trash novels.
4 French wrote 65% of his novel jointly with his computer.
5 French's novel has received mixed reviews.
6 French justifies his action by saying that there is no copyright on the way a person thinks.
7 French doesn't have a publisher for his book yet.
8 AI has traditionally been accepted in the areas of science and engineering.

Task 12 [p.150]

Alone or in pairs, students look at the word or phrase carefully in its context and decide which is the best definition. The teacher checks the answers at class level.

Answers

1	a	5	a
2	b	6	c
3	a	7	a
4	a	8	a

Task 13 [p.151]

Alone or in pairs, students compare the summary with the original and answer the questions. The teacher goes through the summary with the students.

Answers

1 Unimportant details, redundant information, examples, etc. are left out.
2 Information can be joined together by the use of conjunctions, adjectival phrases, relative clauses, etc.
3 There are many possible variations of the summary below but students should ensure that important information is retained.

Example summary

Scott French has cloned the late Jacqueline Susann, a trash novelist, by writing a novel called *Just This Once* in collaboration with his computer. French programmed an AI system with Susann's plots and characterizations to produce a 350-page novel. Not everyone agrees with his methodology.

Some say it violates Susann's rights, but French feels the way a person thinks cannot be copyrighted. A book deal would result in the publication of the first computer-generated novel. AI has hundreds of other applications, both mundane and intriguing. Many of these applications are now outside the traditional fields of science and engineering.

When the summaries are finished, students explain why they cut what they did. If their restructuring is faulty, help them with their new structures.

Task 14 [p.151]

1 diagnosis
2 formula
3 update
4 competitor
5 parallel
6 evaluation
7 franchised
8 clone
9 translation

Hidden word inference

Language focus M

Cause and effect

Exercise 1 [pp.153–154]

Cause
1 Because a modem can be used for inter-computer communication
2 because they are comfortable with what they already have.
3 due to mistakes in the programming or the design.
4 Laser printers can be quite expensive
5 Voice-recognition systems are becoming more sophisticated.

Exercise 2 [p.154]

Effect
1 thereby leaving us with more time for interesting and creative work.
2 you must analyse your needs before making a purchase.
3 it is a good idea to protect sensitive files with a password.
4 so you do not have to buy a fax machine.
5 Computers have been reduced in both size and cost

Exercise 3 [p.154]

2 Because of these and so many other different judgements, there can be no absolute. (Unit 3)
3 Global communication and computer networks will become more and more a part of professional and personal lives as the price of microcomputers and network access drops. (Unit 6)
4 One of the features of a computer virus that separates it from other kinds of computer program is that it replicates itself, so that it can spread to other computers. (Unit 7)
5 ... Lehigh is waiting to infect other unsuspecting computers if you boot from one of those four infected floppies. (Unit 7)
6 As they became more proficient on the computer, some showed gains in their overall self-confidence, as well. (Unit 10)
7 Robots are better at this task, not because they are faster or cheaper than humans, but because they work in a place where humans cannot. (Unit 11)
8 This automatic accuracy is particularly valuable in this kind of industry because locating and fixing mistakes is costly. (Unit 11)
9 Artificial worlds are being built up in a computer memory so that people can walk through at will, look around, and even touch objects. (Unit 12)

14

Multimedia

Task 1 [p.155]

Suggestion 1 The teacher can ask individual students for their opinions and write the information on the board.

Suggestion 2 In pairs or in small groups, students can discuss the questions and take notes. In new pairs or groups, any new information can be added to each student's notes. This can be repeated as often as necessary. Afterwards, the teacher can elicit information from the students and write it on the board.

Example answers

1 Business presentations, training sessions, sales presentations, product introduction, information sessions, etc.
2 The response will depend on each student's knowledge and perception of multimedia. On the 'yes' side, it has so many more possibilities than regular audio-visual systems. On the 'no' side, it is expensive and requires a great deal of preparation.

Task 2 [p.155]

In pairs or small groups, students try to predict the answers using their own knowledge and the information brainstormed in Task 1. If students find it difficult to predict these answers, do not leave too much time for this task. Move on to playing the conversation as soon as the students run out of ideas. Give the students an opportunity to share their ideas with each other before going through the answers at class level.

Tapescript

INTERVIEWER: Nathan, first question: what is multimedia?

NATHAN WARD: Multimedia isn't a thing. It's a capability – like graphics. Just as there are applications that generate graphic images and applications that use graphic images, so there are with multimedia.

INTERVIEWER: OK, but could you give a more specific definition?

NATHAN WARD: I suppose multimedia could be defined as a set of technologies for capturing, manipulating, and presenting information involving different types of data.

INTERVIEWER: What different types of data are involved?

NATHAN WARD: Well, they include audio, image, video, animation, graphics, and text. The data may originate in either digital or analog form.

INTERVIEWER: Can any PC owner adapt his machine for multimedia applications?

NATHAN WARD: Unfortunately, it's not as simple as that. As far as hardware goes, the machine must have colour, a reasonably high-resolution display – say 640 by 480 pixel resolution, plenty of hard disk storage, and a fairly fast processor . . .

INTERVIEWER: How is the audio and video processing done?

NATHAN WARD: I was just coming to that. Audio and video processing is generally still done by add-in circuit boards – or expansion boards, as they're called – so the machine needs slots for those.

INTERVIEWER: Now, I've heard the expression 'full-motion video' being used in connection with multimedia. Isn't video already 'full-motion'?

NATHAN WARD: 'Full-motion video' refers to the impression the viewer has that he or she is watching flicker-free television. The idea is to capture full-motion video in real time and digitize and compress the information so that the system can treat it like any other digital data stream. Some systems do it better than others.

INTERVIEWER: I see. Getting back to hardware requirements, apart from the expansion boards that you mentioned, is there anything else that's needed?

NATHAN WARD: Yes. The machine must have interfaces for a variety of input and output devices.

INTERVIEWER: Such as?

NATHAN WARD: Such as a CD-ROM drive, VCR, digital audio tape . . .

INTERVIEWER: Isn't there a problem of compatibility?

NATHAN WARD: There is, but that situation is changing. Microsoft's base-level MPC specification has some support, but it's only a start. The lack of standards is the main reason that multimedia is not bigger than it is. Once these are in place, users will have easy plug-and-play compatibility, and developers will be able to develop applications that can run on a variety of platforms.

INTERVIEWER: By 'a variety of platforms' you mean IBM PCs, Macs, UNIX and OS/2 workstations, etc.

NATHAN WARD: Exactly. So far, we've only talked about PCs, but workstations are really the ideal platform for multimedia. They have inherent advantages in terms of graphics and power which make them particularly suitable as multimedia authoring machines.

INTERVIEWER: You mean for programmers developing multimedia applications?

NATHAN WARD: Yes.

INTERVIEWER: What is multimedia being used for?

NATHAN WARD: Our research shows that businesses are most interested in multimedia for education and training. That was one of the first areas targeted by developers. But it's also seen as an excellent tool for sales presentations.

INTERVIEWER: What about other applications?

NATHAN WARD: The possibilities are endless. Multimedia is a capability that can be built into products across a variety of market segments, applications, and platforms. In the future, we'll find multimedia in databases, spreadsheets, document processing, e-mail, and many other applications. It'll become as natural to us in our business computing as it is in our home through television and stereo systems.

Example answers

1 Multimedia is similar to graphics because it is a capability. There are applications that generate multimedia, and there are applications that use multimedia.

2 Nathan Ward defines multimedia as a set of technologies for capturing, manipulating, and presenting information involving different types of data.

3 Types of data involved are audio, image, video, animation, graphics, and text.

4 No, it is not easy to adapt most PCs for multimedia applications, because they are often not powerful enough to run multimedia applications.

5 'Full-motion video' refers to the idea viewers have that they are watching flicker-free television.

6 No, there is a lack of industry standards for multimedia.

7 According to Ward, the best platform for multimedia is a workstation.

8 The most popular application of multimedia is education and training.

Task 3 [p.156]

Students listen again to complete the table. The teacher can help by playing only the relevant part of the tape. In pairs or small groups, students can compare their results before checking with the teacher at class level.

Hardware requirements for multimedia

1 colour display
2 reasonably high-resolution display
3 lots of hard disk storage
4 a fairly fast processor
5 expansion boards
6 expansion slots

Task 4 [p.156]

Alone or in pairs, students try to predict the missing words. The teacher then plays the relevant section of the tape while the students check their answers. Finally, in pairs, students can compare their answers before the teacher checks them at class level.

1	viewer	13	drive
2	flicker	14	digital
3	free	15	audio
4	capture	16	compatibility
5	real	17	base
6	time	18	level
7	compress	19	standards
8	stream	20	plug
9	hardware	21	play
10	expansion	22	applications
11	interfaces	23	platforms
12	devices		

Task 5 [pp.157–158]

Students study the sentences before reading the text.

Suggestion 1 Alone, students read the text.

Suggestion 2 Treat this as an interactive reading task, following the procedure described in Suggestion 2, Task 5 (Unit 2), on page 6.

In pairs, students decide which sentence is the best summary, and why. Then, they check with the teacher at class level.

Answer

3 provides the best summary; 1 and 2 provide specific details.

Task 6 [p.158]

Alone or in pairs, students decide whether the statements are true or false, identifying where they think the information appears in the text to justify their answers. The teacher then rounds up at class level making sure students can defend their choices.

1 F (technician doesn't make a mark on it)
2 F (technician calls up the information about the faculty part and the replacement procedure on his workstation)
3 F (change 'computer-generated representation' to 'real-time image')
4 T
5 T
6 T
7 T
8 T

Task 7 [p.158]

Alone or in pairs, students find the answers and check with the teacher at class level.

Answers

1	spots	6	compound
2	procedure	7	infancy
3	tools	8	barriers
4	pops up	9	rudimentary
5	high-end	10	seamlessly

Task 8 [p.159]

The student follow instructions in the Student's Book.

Students can prepare the activity in groups of **A Students** and **B Students** with the teacher offering help where necessary.

Make certain **Student A**s understand what kind of system they have. Check to see that they are able to formulate appropriate questions about price, types of options, etc. Make sure **Student B**s have the information from the listening in Task 3 about system requirements. Check to see that they understand the various products that are offered in the advertisement. When the two groups are fully prepared, they can be paired off to complete the activity. They can repeat the activity as often as necessary. The teacher can challenge the **Student B** group to see who can sell the most products. Don't let the **Student A** group know!

The teacher can present some useful examples of the language of persuasion before beginning the activity, such as *You really should . . ., Why don't you?, Have you thought about . . .?* etc.

Task 9 [p.160]

Students may need guidance from the teacher for this task. Take in other examples of leaflets to give them ideas.

Students work in pairs and use the information from the listening text and from the conversation. If possible, students should prepare their leaflet using word-processing software or even desktop publishing, if it is available. Once all the leaflets are finished, put them on the wall and ask the students to judge which one is the best. They should give their reasons.

Computer-to-video conversion

Task 10 [pp.160–161]

Students read the text and work in pairs to answer the questions. The teacher checks at class level.

Answers

1 On a TV screen, one pass usually writes the entire image. On a computer screen, it will take 50–60 passes. Another difference is the bandwidth.
2 The interlaced video PAL system was invented because there was not enough bandwidth to transmit all 625 lines of one TV image in a fiftieth of a second. The advantage is that it eliminates the flicker for viewing from several yards, but for close-up viewing it could cause a headache.
3 The choice depends on what you want to do with the signal. For example, if you wanted to do word processing, you wouldn't choose the first one. The second suggestion sounds simpler.

Task 11 [p.161]

Alone or in pairs, students can work to complete the task and then check with the teacher at class level.

Answers

1 c	2 a	3 e	4 d	5 b

Task 12 [p.162]

Alone or in pairs, students decide which of the two configurations in the text matches the diagram.

The teacher discusses at class level.

The diagram shows configuration 2. The scan converter is a card which fits into the PC, and a cable is connected from this to the VCR. The scan converter converts the PC standard images to the format accepted by the VCR.

Task 13 [pp.162–163]

1 phenomenon
2 microphone
3 adaptor
4 repair
5 supervisor
6 slot
7 flicker
8 compound
9 scan
10 animation

Language focus N

Making predictions

Exercise 1 [p.166]

Students can use two strategies to find the correct pairs to make complete sentences. One strategy is to match up the verb forms (i.e. present + *will*, past + *would*), and the other is to see that the vocabulary items relate to each other.

Answers

1 d   2 f   3 a   4 b   5 e   6 c

Exercise 2 [p.166]

Again in this exercise, tell students that verb forms and lexical items will help them find the answers.

Answers

1 F   leave/will be
2 F   look at/will get
3 F   wanted/would need
4 F   grows/will be reduced
5 F   installed/would not post

When you ask students to make up six more sentences, review the use of present + *will*, and past + *would*, if necessary. Students could work on this in small groups. You may wish to assign themes from previous units in order to have a variety of vocabulary in these sentences. When the sentences are finished, students can check each other's work for correct verb forms and vocabulary. Then, some students from each group can read their sentences to the rest of the class.

Computer graphics

Task 1 [p.167]

Suggestion 1 The teacher can ask individual students for their opinions and write the information on the board.

Suggestion 2 In pairs or in small groups, students can discuss the questions and take notes. Afterwards, the teacher can elicit information from the students and write it on the board.

Answers

1 The photograph was used in an advertisement for a sore throat remedy.
2 The image was achieved using a graphics package. Three images were scanned in, one normal portrait-shot of the man, one shot with the man's head titled back, and a photograph of a lion's mouth. The images were then combined and retouched.

Task 2 [p.168]

The teacher goes through the pictures at class level, discussing the images and eliciting vocabulary. The students listen to complete the task and compare their answers in pairs. The teacher checks at class level asking students to identify the clues that helped them do the task.

Tapescript

1 Graphics are increasingly being used for medical applications. This computer-generated image shows the major veins and organs of the human body, and is used by doctors who are training medical students. The image was created entirely using a graphics package, rather than using actual medical scans as input.
2 This image was used as an advertisement for a PC business graphics software product. It was created using Tapestry's Quantel Graphics Paintbox. The peacock was photographed several times, and the final image of the bird was made up of various components from each one. The roller-skates were incorporated from a separate shot.

3 This picture shows a series of high-resolution images on screen. The images are displayed using a 24-bit graphics expansion board to drive the monitor. The image of the bird was scanned in from a colour print. Some graphics applications, such as the one used to create the picture of the peacock, allow the manipulation of images at pixel-level.
4 This picture shows another medical application of computer graphics. The screen shows a three-dimensional image of a brain with a tumour on the left. The image is achieved using powerful computer programmes which use two-dimensional scan data as input to create three dimensional images on screen. Such images are also useful to surgeons in planning for reconstructive or cosmetic surgery.
5 This image was output through a high-resolution slide recorder. Business graphics packages, such as the one which created this image, can automatically translate numbers on spreadsheets into a variety of charts and graphs. This kind of package makes it easy for anyone to create clear and effective business graphics for presentations and reports.

Answers

1 b   2 a   3 e   4 d   5 c

Task 3 [p.169]

Alone or in pairs, students match words and definitions. They then check at class level.

Answers

1 c   2 e   3 d   4 b   5 a

Task 4 [pp.169–170]

Alone or in pairs or small groups, students try to find as many differences as possible, keeping a note of them for discussion at class level. Encourage them to guess why the changes were made.

Note that the slogan *Now there's light at the end of the tunnel*, is a play on words. The expression means that soon there is going to be a change for the better (i.e. Virgin Atlantic will be flying out of Heathrow).

Task 5 [p.171]

In pairs, students read the text carefully to find the alterations made in the creation of the poster. Encourage students to suggest reasons for changes even if those reasons are not given in the text.

Answers

The answers in brackets are suggested reasons and are not actually stated in the text.

Alteration	Reason
■ vehicles leaving tunnel removed	(too many cars leaving)
■ cars on opposite side replaced	(to show private/public transport)
■ Toshiba ad/Welcome to Heathrow	(to show location)
■ other ad and steps removed	(to give better composition)
■ bush redrawn	out of character; too spiky
■ streetlights extended	because of inclusion of airliner
■ shadow added to airliner	because of position of light
■ light added to end of tunnel	to match the slogan
■ lorry added disappearing into light	(to add realism)

Task 6 [p.171]

Alone, in pairs, or in groups of three, students can formulate questions on the text, then have them checked by the teacher. Then, they can work with a partner, or regroup and repeat the activity until the teacher is satisfied.

Example answers

1 When was the poster and press campaign being put together?
2 Who knew some kind of electronic trickery would be required?
3 Who makes the electronic Dalim Litho design system?
4 Why was this ad being designed?
5 Was the shot of the tunnel taken at Gatwick?
6 Why did considerable retouching take place?
7 What replaced the Toshiba ad?
8 Why was a patch of light created at the end of the tunnel?

Task 7 [p.171]

Alone or in pairs, students can complete this activity by referring back to the text for the correct word reference. Then, they can check their answers with another student or pair, or with the teacher.

1 inherent   5 neighbouring
2 dips   6 shadow
3 conventional   7 elusive
4 rank   8 wasted

24-bit colour

Task 8 [pp.172–173]

Alone or in pairs, students try to answer the questions. The teacher can round up at class level or go straight on to the reading.

Alone, students read the text, and in pairs or small groups find the answers to the questions, checking if they are the same as their answers. The teacher rounds up at class level.

Answers

1 Between 150 and 200 shades.
2 a A single dot on a computer screen, usually a square of a single colour.
  b A binary mathematical digit, i.e. a switch that can have two possible values, 0 or 1 (formed from two words BInary and digiT).
  c A group of eight bits.
  d A monochrome monitor that can display all shades of grey from black to white.
3 16.7 million colour shades.
4 Three megabytes of memory.

Task 9 [p.173]

Alone or in pairs, students decide whether the statements are true or false and identify where they think the information appears in the text to justify their answers. They then make the necessary changes to the false statements.

The teacher then elicits responses from around the class to check, making sure students can give line references to support their answers.

Answers

1 T
2 F
3 T
4 F
5 F (it offers 256 levels of transparency)
6 T

Task 10 [p.174]

Alone or in pairs, students do this exercise. The teacher should encourage them to use their own words by finding synonyms or equivalent expressions and by summarizing portions of the original text. The teacher checks the answers with the class, discussing the appropriateness of different answers.

Example answers

A Would you like some information on any of our hardware or software packages?

A What would you like to know?

A You will get full colour photographic quality with up to 16.7 million colour shades.

A You'll need a special plug-in circuit board to drive your monitor.

A What kind of screen do you have?

A Then you'll need three megabytes of memory to drive the screen.

A No, it isn't really. For your applications, an 8-bit colour monitor is sufficient.

Task 11 [p.174]

Students will come up with many variations for this task. Make sure that the main ideas of the text are in the summary. If you feel some ideas ideas are missing from a student's text, ask the students to explain why he or she left that detail out.

Task 12 [pp.174–175]

Across		Down	
2	acoustic coupler	1	scramble
4	inkjet	2	arithmetic-logic
5	analog	3	radiation screen
6	signal	10	signs off
7	expert		
8	standard		
9	function		
11	cyborg		
12	infect		
13	access		
14	delete		
15	control function		

Appendix 1
Letter writing

1 Presentation and structure

All the tasks in this section can be done as individual, pair, or group work. If teachers have access to overhead projectors, letters can be written on transparencies by groups of students, then projected on a wall or screen. This allows the whole class to comment on, correct, and improve each other's letters. The teacher can amend each letter to incorporate the students' suggestions, then photocopy the transparencies and distribute them to the students who created them.

Task

1	F	6	F
2	T	7	T
3	T	8	T
4	F	9	F
5	T (if you know it)	10	F

2 Enquiries and replies

Task 1

1	g	4	j	7	a	10	k
2	e	5	h	8	b	11	d
3	f	6	i	9	c		

Task 2

1	for	4	in	7	to	10	with
2	of	5	From	8	on	11	on
3	in	6	for	9	to	12	from

Task 3

1	d	4	c	7	c	10	b
2	c	5	a	8	d		
3	c	6	d	9	c		

Task 4

a	9	d	6	g	4	j	2
b	10	e	5	h	3		
c	8	f	1	i	7		

Task 5

The students can write this letter using the letter in Task 1 on page 178 as a model. Letters will vary, but they should contain all the information requested.

Task 6

Students can use the letter of enquiry in Task 4 on pages 180–181 as a model.

3 Quotations and orders

Before starting the tasks, take students through the glossary of terms on page 187. Encourage students to refer to this as necessary while they are doing the tasks.

Task 1

quantity	*initial*	*allow*
made	*on*	*assure*

Task 2

Encourage students to modify their books with the correct version, so that they have a good model for this kind of letter.

Answers
1 Dear *Mr Wilson* (no initials).
2 Please *find* enclosed . . . (not *found*).
3 We would like *to confirm* that . . . (not *confirming*).
4 will *be made* by . . . (not *make*).
5 We would appreciate *it* if . . . (*if* missing).
6 I look forward to *hearing* from . . . (not *hear*).
7 shortly (not *in short*).
8 Yours *sincerely* (not *faithfully*).

Task 3

VAT, pronounced as a word or as initials, means *value added tax*. This is a tax on the rise in value of a product at each stage of its manufacture.

Answers

1 g	4 a	7 d	10 c
2 h	5 i	8 f	
3 j	6 b	9 e	

Task 4

a 11	d 12	g 8	j 1
b 10	e 5	h 6	k 9
c 2	f 3	i 4	l 7

Task 5

1 how you would like us to pay?
2 how many items you would like to order.
3 whether you have the items in stock?
4 whether these terms are acceptable to you.
5 whether you anticipate any delays with delivery.
6 when you would be able to ship the order.
7 where you would like us to send the order.
8 whether you would be prepared to offer us a quantity discount?
9 when you would like to receive payment.
10 whether you would like us to arrange a maintenance contract.

Task 6

The students will have to refer back to Section 2, Enquiries and replies, to find models for the first two paragraphs. The teacher should ensure that students lay their letters out correctly, incorporating addresses, dates, etc.

4 Letters of complaint and replies

Task 1

1 Yes.
2 The machines he ordered were loaded with the wrong version of DOS, and some cables were missing.
3 He wants the supplier to send a representative to install the correct version of DOS. He also wants him to send the missing cables as soon as possible.
4 Yes. The letter is firm but polite.

Task 2

1 for	4 to	7 on	10 out
2 of	5 from/out of	8 on	11 for
3 with	6 in	9 at	

Task 3

1 The wrong items have been sent to us again.
2 This consignment should have been delivered last week.
3 Two of the VDUs were broken during transportation.
4 The order was sent by sea mail instead of air mail.
5 Please let me know when you think this matter can be sorted out.
6 The documents should have been sent by registered post.
7 The problems with the hard disk could have been caused by a faulty connection.
8 The manuals were omitted from the order.
9 The printers were delivered over three weeks late.
10 The invoice will not be paid until this problem is rectified.

Task 4

1 e	3 d	5 g	7 c
2 f	4 a	6 h	8 b

Task 5

In order to be able to answer question 1, the students must first be sure of the purpose of the letter. The teacher should encourage them to decide on the writer's intentions before they judge the letter.

Example answers
1a The purpose of the letter is to remind the supplier of his obligation, and to ensure that the order is sent without delay. The letter therefore fails on a number of counts:
  1 It contains no reference to the specific order.
  2 It rambles (i.e. the writer says in 150 words what he could have said in 80 words).
  3 It is offensive. The supplier may not even be responsible for the delay. In any case, he will be unlikely to make any special effort to despatch the order after receiving a letter like this.
b By putting right the failings mentioned in **1a** above.
2 I am writing to complain about the late delivery of the software protection plugs we ordered from you in order no.—.

  May I remind you that prompt delivery was stated as a firm condition of the order, as we were planning to market the product at the end of November.

  Please ensure that the order is delivered within the next five days, or we shall have to look for an alternative supplier.

  I look forward to hearing from you.